INDIAN INSTANT POT Cookbook

Easy, Healthy Traditional Indian Recipes Anyone Can Cook at Home

Brandon Hearn

Contents

Introduction

This recipe book provides a complete guideline to cook and prepare certain food items. An ideal recipe consists of a title, cooking time, nutrition info, ingredients to cook and step-by-step cooking procedures with some notes and tips.

This book was written by following the above guidelines. Each recipe in this book has the standard form of an ideal recipe.

The main purpose of this book is to help the people who love to cook or who are bored with common recipes and cannot spend much time only cooking. As the instant pot is the easiest way of cooking and this equipment can cook an item more quickly than in general, we choose different recipes that can be made by instant pot for this book.

This book consists 101 Indian instant pot recipes with a lot of variety such as Main dishes; side dishes, desserts, and breakfast, etc. the recipes are also categorized by vegetables, chicken, beef, rice, etc. so that you can easily find the recipe you are looking for.

So, let's have a look at the recipes and find the recipe you want to cook.

WHAT IS AN INSTANT POT

This useful device can do a lot of things—and it could be freaking fast cooking. Instant Pot is simple enough for a kid to use it, and you can be sure it can be the best help to you in your kitchen. In addition to cooking meals like meat, chicken, beef, and dried beans at lightning speed, it also possible cook yogurts and rise meals. We can easily call it the just Only #1 Pot instead of the Instant Pot, since it's the only cooking device you need.

All of which means one very important thing: Cooking healthy, easy, mouthwatering meals has never been easier.

Once you have a full understanding of what the electric pressure cooker is and what it can do, you are going to fall in love with your newfound freedom in the kitchen. I am not joking, it's true.

The Instant Pot is a combination of seven different kitchen gadgets, and it can do far more than any one of those gadgets ever does on their own. Of course, this pressure cooker is very intimidating and can be downright confusing at first, but with a little instruction, you will know what you're doing.

The basic Instant Pot comes with the unit itself, a lid, an interior pot, a plastic piece to collect condensation, a trivet and utensils. Assembling the unit is very intuitive, you plug in the power cord, place the interior pot into the Instant Pot, place the lid on top and you are good to go. You will find the spot for the condensation collector to slide into place on the back of the Instant Pot, near the base. In general, you will not see much condensation collect back here, it is only for heavy flow scenarios.

The lid of the Instant Pot warrants a closer look as you will frequently be dealing with the steamer function which will, in turn, require caution as the steam will easily be hot enough to cause burns that may not be serious, but will certainly be painful. To lock the lid, you are going to move the steam release handle into the sealing position. The top of the lid also features a float valve that pushes up from inside of the lid. This valve will be down when the Instant Pot is not at maximum pressure which serves as a visual indicator as to if it is safe to open or not.

Inside of the lid you will see where the float valve connects, along with the exhaust valve which is covered to keep it working properly. You will want to practice removing the covering of the exhaust valve before you use the Instant Pot to ensure you know what you are doing before it needs cleaning. Regular cleaning of the exhaust valve is key to ensuring your Instant Pot remains at peak functionality. Occasionally, you will also need to clean the float valve, to do so you will need to remove the silicone covering beforehand, it should come off easily as long as it is cleaned regularly.

The inside of the lid also features a sealing ring, which sits in a metal rack that can also be removed for cleaning purposes. It is important to be extremely careful with this sealing ring as if it is stretched or altered in anyway, it will be impossible for the Instant Pot to generate a reliable seal, severely limiting its versatility. The lid can also be propped open by simply inserting one of the fins into the notch in the handle on the base of the Instant Pot.

In order to close the Instant Pot securely, all you need to do is to place the lid on the unit so the arrows on the cooker and the arrows on the lid line up. Turning the lid will then align the arrow on the lid to align with the closed lock picture on the base. This will require a clockwise movement and will be accompanied by a chime if the unit is plugged in. Opening the Instant Pot requires a counter-clockwise movement and will also be accompanied by a chime if the unit is plugged in.

How to Use the Buttons on the Instant Pot

Keep Warm/Cancel Button

This button is self-explanatory. You press this button to either cancel a cooking function or if you want to switch off your Instant Pot. You can also click on the Adjust button to increase and even reduce the heat of the Pot.

Sauté Button

This function is to sauté your ingredients inside the pot, just as how you sauté things in a pot. You can also click the Adjust button and Sauté button for more charring and to a simmer, you press the Adjust and Sauté button twice.

Manual Button

This button has an all-purpose function. If your recipe mentions cooking on high-pressure for a specific cook time- use this button. You can adjust the cooking time with the '+' or '-indicators. There are also pre-set buttons that you can use instead of the manual one. Most pressure cooking recipes already come with instructions on how many hours and minutes you need to cook a meal for. But with the Instant Cooker Pot, it makes your life easier if in the event you do not have any available recipes or if you want to build or make something from scratch. The preset buttons guide you into determining the amount of time needed for an individual meal.

Here's a list of these buttons and what they can do for pressure cooking:

To make soup

For delicious soups, pressure-cook them on high for 30 minutes cook time. All you need to do is put all your ingredients in the pot, press the 'Soup' time and the 'Adjust' button once (more) increase cook time to forty minutes. If you want to cook for twenty minutes, press 'Soup' and 'Adjust' twice (less) to cook for less time. No more slaving over the stove to make the perfect soup.

For meat & stews

High-pressure cook time is required for 35 minutes for meats and stews, so the meat drops off the bone. To adjust more, click on Adjust more to cook for 45 minutes and to cook less, adjust less to cook for 20 minutes.

For Beans & Chili

A 30-minute cook time on high-pressure is required. To add more time, press 'Adjust' '+' to increase to 45 minutes and '- 'to decrease to 25 minutes. The Instant Pot cuts the time in half when making chili.

For Poultry

You want the meat tender but not too flaky so the cook time for this is 15 minutes of high pressure. Of course, you can adjust to a 30-minute cook time with '+' or 25-minute cook time with '-.'

For Rice

Rice needs to be fluffy. Too much water and it's lumpy and too little water will make your rice undercooked and dry. The rice function is the only fully automatic programming on the Instant Pot Cooker.

The electronic programming adjusts cooking time depending on the ratio of water and rice that you put in the cooking pot.

For Multi-Grain

Ideal to be cooked on high pressure for 40 minutes cook time. If you need to soak them, and then adjust the timer to 45 minutes soaking and 60 minutes cook time.

For Porridge and Congee

The texture you are looking for is soft and somewhat lumpy. Cook on high pressure for 20 minutes. To add more tie, press Adjust '+' to cook for 30 minutes. For less adjust '-for 15 min cook time.

For Steaming

Use a steamer basket or a rack for this function because you want to prevent the food from having to touch the bottom of the pot when it heats at full power.

You can cook on high pressure for just 10 minutes. Once the pot reaches the desired pressure, the steam button automatically regulates pressure. Use the '+' or '-buttons to adjust cook time or use the Pressure button to change the fixed timing for lower or higher temperature.

Apart from the buttons above, you also have on your Instant Pot Cooker:

The Instant Pot switch which is set to default to a four-hour slow cooking time.

You can adjust the buttons to slow cook at 190 to 210-degree Fahrenheit for low pressure, 194 to 205-degree Fahrenheit to normal pressure and 199 to 210-degree Fahrenheit for high pressure. Again use, the "+" and "-" buttons to adjust the cooking time accordingly to your desired doneness.

The Pressure button which switches to low or high pressure.

The Yogurt button to make amazing homemade yogurt and can be set to low or high pressure.

The Timer button which is ideal for delayed cooking. Depending on what you are cooking, you need to select a cooking function first, and the make the necessary adjustments. Next, press the timer button and the adjust button to set more or less cook time with then "+" and "-" buttons.

Rice Recipes

Delicious Express Biryani

Overall cooking time: 40 min

Serving: 5

Nutrition info: Calories: 273, Fat: 8g, Carbs: 22g, Protein: 18g.

Ingredients:

Marinated chicken	4-6 legs
Ghee	4 Tbsp.
Bay leaves	2
Cardamom	2
Onion	3, sliced
Ginger-garlic paste	2 Tbsp.
Basmati rice	2 cups
Mint leaves	2 handfuls
Cilantro	2 handfuls
Salt	3/4 Tbsp.
Saffron	2 pinches

Cooking procedure:

1. First, soak the rice in a large bowl with 2 cups of water for 20 minutes.

2. Then go to the sauté function on the instant pot and add the ghee. When the ghee is hot, add the bay leaves and cardamom, then add the onion and sauté for 2 to 3 minutes. Sprinkle a pinch of salt here and add the ginger paste. Sauté for 10 minutes.

3. Now gently add the marinated chicken to the instant pot and set the time manually to 5 minutes at high pressure.

4. Meanwhile drain the rice and rinse slightly. When the cooking is done, open the lid and pour the rice into the instant pot with a cup of fresh water. Add the remaining ghee, salt, and other ingredients.

5. Close the lid and manually set the time for 5 minutes at high pressure.

6. You can also garnish with raisins and cashews.

Quick Beetroot Rice

Overall cooking time: 30 min

Serving: 3

Nutrition info: Calories: 150, Fat: 0g, Carbs: 13g, Protein: 3.5g.

Ingredients:

Basmati rice	1 cup
Water	1 ¼ cups
Ghee	1 Tbsp.
Cumin seeds	½ tsp.
Ginger paste	½ tsp.
Garlic paste	½ tsp.
Onion	1/2, sliced
Beet	1, cut into small pieces
Green peas	½ cup
Lemon juice	1 Tbsp.
Spices	2 Tbsp.
Salt	2 tsp.

Cooking procedure:

1. Set the sauté function in the instant pot, add the ghee, spices and cumin seeds, and sauté for 30 seconds.

2. Add the onion, garlic and ginger. Sauté for 2 minutes.

3. Now add the rice, beets, peas and other ingredients. Stir to mix well.

4. Close the lid and manually set the time for 4 minutes at high pressure.

5. Release the pressure manually for 10 minutes and then quick release. Open the lid and add the lemon juice.

6. Fluff   and   serve.

Easy Basmati Rice

Overall cooking time: 10 min

Serving: 2

Nutrition info: Calories: 180, Fat: 0.5g, Carbs: 38g, Protein: 5.5g.

Ingredients:

Rice   1 cup
Water 1 cup

Cooking procedure:

1. Take your instant pot and place the rice into it. Pour in 1 cup of water.
2. Close the lid and manually set the time for 6 minutes at high pressure.
3. When the cooking is done, naturally release the pressure for 10 minutes and then do a quick release.
4. Fluff the rice and enjoy.

Jeera/cumin Rice

Overall cooking time: 20 min

Serving: 2

Nutrition info: Calories: 305, Fat: 4g, Carbs: 65g, Protein: 5g.

Ingredients:

Basmati rice	1 cup
Water	1 ¼ cups
Cumin seeds	1 Tbsp.
Salt	1 Tbsp.
Ghee	1 Tbsp.
Spices	as you like

Cooking procedure:

1. Switch your instant pot to sauté and place one tablespoon ghee in it.

2. When it is heated, add the spices, ingredients and the cumin seeds. Sauté for 1 minute.

3. Now add the rinsed rice and the water. Close the lid and manually set the time for 4 minutes at high pressure.

4. When the cooking is done, naturally release the pressure for 5 minutes and then do a quick release.

5. Open the lid and sprinkle the salt over the rice. Fluff well.

Healthy Vegetable Rice

Overall cooking time: 30 min

Serving: 4-5

Nutrition info: Calories: 250, Fat: 4g, Carbs: 50g, Protein: 6.6g.

Ingredients:

Olive oil	1 Tbsp.
Chopped shallot	¼ cup
Garlic	1 clove
Basmati rice	1 ½ cups
Copped carrot	½ cup
Kosher salt	1 tsp.
Curry powder	2 Tbsp.
Chicken broth	2 cups
Frozen peas	1 cup

Cooking procedure:

1. Switch on the instant pot to sauté and add the olive oil to the metal pan. Then add the onion and sauté for 2 minutes. Then add the garlic and rice. Stir occasionally.

2. Now add the chicken broth, curry powder, carrots and salt. Stir to combine well.

3. Close the lid and manually set the time for 22 minutes at high pressure.

4. When the cooking is done, naturally release the pressure for 10 minutes and then do a quick release.
5. Fluff the rice and serve immediately.

Delicious Rice Pilaf

Overall cooking time: 25 min

Serving: 4

Nutrition info: Calories: 160, Fat: 3.5g, Carbs: 30g, Protein: 3g.

Ingredients:

Rice	2 cups
Chicken stock	2 cups
Rice wine	1 Tbsp.
Vegetable oil	1 Tbsp.
Leftover meat	1 cup
Waxy potatoes	2, cubed
Carrots	2, chopped
White mushrooms	1 lb.
Green beans	1 lb.
Kale with stems	3 cups
Soy sauce	2 Tbsp.
Oyster sauce	1 Tbsp.

Cooking procedure:

1. Take your instant pot and place the rice, vegetables, rice wine and chicken stock. On top of the rice, place the potatoes, meat, carrots, mushrooms, kale and green beans. Lastly spread the soy sauce on the top.
2. Close the lid and manually set the time for 8 minutes at high pressure. Do not use the RICE function.
3. When the cooking is done, naturally release the pressure for 10 minutes and then do a quick release.

4. Stir slowly and gently
mix the rice well.

Tasty Cabbage Rice

Overall cooking time: 25 min

Serving: 8

Nutrition info: Calories: 280, Fat: 9g, Carbs: 45g, Protein: 7g.

Ingredients:

Basmati rice	2 cups	Ginger grated	2 Tbsp.
Olive oil	2 Tbsp.	Chilies	4, minced
Asafetida	¼ Tbsp.	Cabbage	4 cups
Mustard seeds	1 Tbsp.	Salt	2 Tbsp.
Peanuts	½ cup	Lemon juice	2 Tbsp.
Turmeric	½ Tbsp.	Cilantro	½ cup
Curry leaves	15	Coconut grated	3 Tbsp.,

Cooking procedure:

1. Set the instant pot to sauté temperature and add the olive oil. When the olive oil is heated, add the mustard seeds and asafetida. Pop them properly.

2. Then add peanuts and sauté for 1 minute more and then add the green chilies, ginger, turmeric and curry leaves. Mix and cook to brown the peanuts.

3. Now add the cabbage, salt and drained rice to the instant pot. Add 2 cups of water, close the lid, and press the RICE function of the instant pot.

4. When the cooking is done, naturally release the pressure for 10 minutes and then quick release.

5. Open the lid and fluff the rice with lemon juice. Before serving, garnish with coconut and cilantro.

Delicious Kemma Polao

Overall cooking time: 30 min
Serving: 3
Nutrition info: Calories: 468, Fat: 12g,
Carbs: 65g, Protein: 22g.

Ingredients:

Lean lamb	1 lb. minced
Olive oil	4 Tbsp.
Onion	1/2, chopped
Garlic	3 cloves, minced
Ginger	1 Tbsp.
Tomato	1, chopped
Tomato diced	2 plum
Chili sauce	1 Tbsp.
Green chilies	2 Tbsp.
Oregano	½ Tbsp.
Basmati rice	2 cups
Ghee	1 Tbsp.
Spices	2 Tbsp.
Vegetable mix	2-3 cups

Cooking procedure:

1. Go to the sauté function and add the onion with oil and whole spices. Sauté until the onion is translucent.

2. Then add the minced lamb and brown it for 10 minutes. Add the salt, oregano, coriander powder, paprika, pepper,

garam masala, ginger, garlic and cinnamon. Cook for 5 minutes.

3. Now add the other ingredients except the rice. Fry for 5 minutes more. Then add the rice and 4 cups of hot water. Close the lid and manually set the time for 10 minutes at high pressure.

4. When the cooking is done, naturally release the pressure for 10 minutes and then do a quick release.

5. Open the lid and fluff the polao

Spinach Rice with Indian flavors

Overall cooking time: 20 minutes.

Serving: 3

Nutrition info: Calories: 160, Fat: 8g, Carbs: 20g, Protein: 6g.

Ingredients:

Long grain rice	2 cups
Chicken broth	2 cups
Frozen spinach	16 oz. thawed & pressed
Garam masala	2 Tbsp.
Salt	½ tsp.

Cooking procedure:

1. First, squeeze as much water out of the spinach as you can and then mix with chicken broth.

2. Take your instant pot and add the rice and the mixed broth in the pressure cooker. Add the salt and masala.

3. Close the lid and manually set the time for 8 minutes at high pressure.

4. When the cooking is done, do a quick release.

5. Open the lid and fluff the rice.

Tasty Cajun Rice

Overall cooking time: 25 min

Serving: 2

Nutrition info: Calories: 140, Fat: 4g, Carbs: 19g, Protein: 6g.

Ingredients:

Olive oil   1 tsp.
Onion   1, diced
Basmati rice 1 cup
Chili powder ½ tsp.
Thyme   1/3 tsp.
Oregano   1/3 tsp.
Paprika   ½ tsp.
Cumin   ½ tsp.
Vegetable   1 ½ cups, frozen
Tomato puree   2 Tbsp.
Salt, lime & coriander to taste.

Cooking procedure:

1. Set the sauté function in the instant pot and add the oil. Add the onion and sauté until brown.
2. Now add the rice, the spices, other ingredients, and the vegetables too. Stir to mix.
3. Close the lid and manually set the time for 4 minutes at high pressure.
4. When the cooking is done, do a quick release.
5. Open the lid and fluff with lime juice, black pepper and salt.

Easy White Rice

Overall cooking time: 10 min

Serving: 4

Nutrition info: Calories: 138, Fat: 0.2g, Carbs: 31g, Protein: 3g.

Ingredients:

Raw rice	1 cup
Salt	to taste

Cooking procedure:

1. Soak the rice for at least 30 minutes and then add to the instant pot.
2. Add ½ cup of water and salt with the rice. Now close the lid and manually set the time to 5 minutes at medium pressure.
3. Quick release the pressure and fluff before serving.

Chicken Recipes

Homemade Chicken Korma

Overall cooking time: 25 min

Serving: 4

Nutrition info: Calories: 324, Fat: 17g, Carbs: 13g, Protein: 33g.

Ingredients:

For the sauce:

Raw almonds	1 oz.
Onion	1, chopped
Tomato	½ cup, diced
Serrano chili	½
Ginger	1 Tbsp.
Turmeric	1 Tbsp.
Salt	1 tsp.
Garam masala	1 Tbsp.
Cumin	1 Tbsp.
Coriander	1 Tbsp.
Cayenne pepper	½ tsp.

For the korma:

Chicken breasts	1 lb.
Coconut milk	½ cup
Garam masala	1 Tbsp.
Tomato paste	1 Tbsp.
Cilantro	¼ Tsp.

Cooking procedure:

1. First, make the sauce by blending the almond, garlic, ginger, serrano, tomato, turmeric, salt, masala, cumin, cayenne, coriander and onion with 1 cup of water.

2. Now add the sauce to the instant pot and place the chicken breasts on top. Close the lid and manually set the time for 10 minutes at high pressure.

3. When the cooking is done, naturally release the pressure for 10 minutes and then do a quick release.
4. Open the lid and cut the chicken into small pieces. Return to the pot and add the coconut milk, tomato paste and garam masala.
5. Garnish and serve.

Delicious Mom's Curry

Overall cooking time: 35 min
Serving: 3
Nutrition info: Calories: 240, Fat: 15g,
Carbs: 16g, Protein: 7g.

Ingredients:

Boneless chicken breasts	1 lb.
Ghee	3 Tbsp.
Chili	1
Ginger	1 inch, chopped
Garlic	5 cloves
Onion	1, chopped
Tomatoes	2, chopped
Lemon juice	1 tsp.

Cooking procedure:

1. Set the instant pot to sauté mode and add the oil. Add the spices and sauté to get aroma.
2. Then add the onion, garlic, ginger and chili and sauté for 4 minutes.
3. Now add the tomatoes, stir and add the chicken. Sauté everything for 2 minutes more.
4. Close the lid and manually set the time for 5 minutes at high pressure.
5. When the cooking is done, do a quick release.
6. Open the lid and fluff with the lemon juice.

Delicious Apricot Chicken

Overall cooking time: 30 min
Serving: 4
Nutrition info: Calories: 328, Fat: 13g, Carbs: 29g, Protein: 28g.

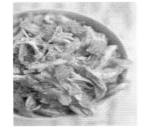

Ingredients:

Chicken thighs	2 ½ lbs.
Salt	½ tsp.
Black pepper	¼ tsp.
Vegetable oil	1 Tbsp.
Onion	1, chopped
Chicken broth	½ cup
Ginger	1 Tbsp.
Garlic	2 cloves
Cinnamon	½ tsp.
Allspice	1/8 tsp.
Tomatoes	1 can, diced
Apricots	8-ounce can

Cooking procedure:

1. First, season the chicken with salt and pepper and sauté with oil in your instant pot until brown. Set aside.

2. Now add the onion and sauté for 3 minutes. Then add the ginger, cilantro, spices and garlic. Stir for 30 seconds and add the tomatoes, apricots and chicken broth. Mix and return the chicken to the pot.

3. Close the lid and manually set the time for 12 minutes at high pressure.

4. When the cooking is done, naturally release the pressure for 10 minutes and then do a quick release.

5. Open the lid and fluff with the extra salt and pepper. Serve with parsley garnish.

Spicy Chicken Curry

Overall cooking time: 45 min
Serving: 6
Nutrition info: Calories: 310, Fat: 22g, Carbs: 15g, Protein: 19g.

Ingredients:

Butter	3 Tbsp.
Bay leaf	1
Cinnamon stick	2 inch
Cumin seeds	½ tsp.
Onion	2 cups, chopped
Garlic	1 Tbsp.
Ginger	1 Tbsp.
Tomato paste	2 Tbsp.
Coriander powder	1 ½ tsp.
Turmeric powder	¾ Tbsp.
Chili powder	¾ Tbsp.
Salt	1 Tbsp.
Chicken thighs	3 lbs.
Potato	2 cups, cubed
Chicken broth	½ cup
Garam masala	1 Tbsp.

Cooking procedure:

1. First, go to the sauté function, melt the butter and then add the bay leaf, cinnamon and cumin seeds. Fragrant gently.

2. Then add the garlic, ginger and the onion. Sauté for 5 minutes. Here, add the tomato paste and cook for 3 minutes with 2 Tbsp. of water.

3. Add the other ingredients and stir. Lastly add the chicken and the chicken broth.

4. Close the lid, press the POULTRY mode, and adjust the time to 15 minutes.

5. Yap, it's ready. Garnish as you like.

Homemade Chicken Dopiaza

Overall cooking time: 45 min

Serving: 2

Nutrition info: Calories: 250, Fat: 14g, Carbs: 5g, Protein: 25g.

Ingredients:

Onion	1 ½ cups	Cumin	2 Tbsp.
Garlic	4 cloves	Turmeric	1 Tbsp.
Ginger	20 gm	Chicken	1 lb.
Chili pepper	3	Fenugreek leaf	1 Tbsp.
Ghee	2 Tbsp.	Tomato paste	2 Tbsp.
Cardamom pods	3	Dark brown sugar	1 tsp.
Chili powder	1 tsp.	Salt	1 tsp.
Coriander	1 Tbsp.	Garam masala	1 Tbsp.

Cooking procedure:

1. First, add one-third of the onion with garlic and ginger to a blender and blend to paste.

2. Turn on the sauté function and add the two-thirds of the onion with 1 Tbsp. of ghee and sauté for 3 minutes. Set aside.

3. Now, add the rest of the ghee to the instant pot with the garlic-onion paste and sauté for 2 minutes. Add the cardamom pods, cumin, turmeric and chili powders. Stir for 30 seconds.

4. Add the meat and stir to coat. Add the other ingredients. Secure the lid and manually set the cooking time to 10 minutes at high pressure. Allow to cook.

5. When it is done, allow 7 minutes natural release and then do a quick release.

6. Separate the meat from the instant pot and sauté the sauce for half an hour. Place the meat back into the instant pot and add the fried onion and leave that with high temperature for few min.

Delicious Butter Chicken

Overall cooking time: 30 min
Serving: 6
Nutrition info: Calories: 542, Fat:
16g, Carbs: 59g, Protein: 60g.

Ingredients:

Chicken thighs	2 lbs.
Ghee	2 Tbsp.
Tandoori masala	¼ cup
Ginger	2 inches
Garlic	4 cloves
Kosher salt	1 pinch
Plain yogurt	1 cup
Sauce	1 ½ cup

Cooking procedure:

1. In a mixing bowl, add the yogurt, salt, tandoori masala, ginger and garlic. Mix. Now add the chicken and marinate both sides well with the mixture. Transfer to the refrigerator for 1 hour to overnight.

2. Go to the sauté function and sauté the onion in the ghee for 3 minutes and then add the other ingredients. Lastly, add the marinated chicken and the chicken broth. Add the refrigerated marinade at the top of the chicken.

3. Close the lid and manually set the time for 12 minutes at high pressure.

4. When the cooking is done, naturally release the pressure for 10 minutes and then do a quick release.

5. Open the lid, pour in the evaporated milk with the cilantro, and stir to mix properly.

Spices Chicken Korma

Overall cooking time: 25 min
Serving: 6
Nutrition info: Calories: 324, Fat: 15g, Carbs: 13g, Protein: 32g.

Ingredients:

Chicken	1 lb.
Onion	1, chopped
Tomatoes	½ cup, diced
Garlic	5 cloves
Ginger	1 Tbsp.
Salt	1 Tbsp.
Garam masala	1 Tbsp.
Cumin seeds	1 tsp.
Spices	3 Tbsp.
Coconut milk	½ cup
Cilantro	¼ cup

Cooking procedure:

1. First, pour the spices in a blender. Add the cumin seeds, garlic, ginger, onion and tomatoes. Blend well.

2. Now, pour the sauce into the instant pot and then add the chicken on the top of the sauce.

3. Close the lid and manually set the time for 12 minutes at high pressure.

4. When the cooking is done, naturally release the pressure for 10 minutes and then do a quick release.

5. Open the lid and cut the chicken into bite-size pieces.

6. Add the coconut milk and stir. Add back the chicken and combine.

Homemade Chicken Tikka Masala

Overall cooking time: 30 min

Serving: 4

Nutrition info: Calories: 360,
Fat: 14g, Carbs: 37g, Protein: 21g.

Ingredients:

Olive oil	2 Tbsp.
Onion	1, chopped
Garlic cloves	3, minced
Ginger	1 inch
Paprika	2 Tbsp.
Garam masala	1 Tbsp.
Turmeric	1 tsp.
Cumin	2 Tbsp.

Coriander	1 Tbsp.
Pepper	¼ Tbsp.
Tomatoes	14 oz. diced
Chicken breast skinless	1 ½ lbs.
Chicken broth	½ cup
Coconut milk	½ cup
Lemon juice	2 tbsp

Cooking procedure:

1. Turn on the sauté function of your instant pot and add the olive oil. Once the pot is hot, sauté the onion with garlic and ginger for 3 minutes.

2. Then cancel the sauté function and add the spices, ingredients and tomatoes. Stir to combine and then add the chicken on top. Pour in the chicken broth.

3. Close the lid and manually set the time for 7 minutes at high pressure. Allow to cook.

4. When the cooking is done, release the pressure and open the lid. Take out the chicken breasts and chop. You can use a fork to do that. Place the chicken back in the instant pot.

5. Go back to the sauté function and simmer for 5 minutes more. Add the other ingredients. When the mixture is thickened enough to satisfy you stop cooking.

Delicious Chicken Masala

Overall cooking time: 30 min

Serving: 8

Nutrition info: Calories: 140, Fat: 1.6g, Carbs: 11g, Protein: 18g.

Ingredients:

Whole chicken	1
Onion	1, chopped
Avocado oil	2 Tbsp.
Ghee	1 Tbsp.
Cumin seeds	1 tsp.
Garlic paste	1 Tbsp.
Ginger paste	1 Tbsp.
Turmeric powder	1 Tbsp.
Garam masala	3 Tbsp.
Salt	2 Tbsp.
Chili powder	½ Tbsp.
Tomato	3 Tbsp. crushed
Plain yogurt	2 Tbsp.
Bay leaf	1

Cooking procedure:

1. Go to the sauté function in your instant pot and add the oil first. Once the oil heated, add the onion and sauté for 3 minutes. Then add the garlic and ginger paste. Sauté for another minute.

2. Now add the chicken and sauté for 5 minutes while continuously stirring. Then add all the other ingredients.

3. Secure the lid and manually set the time to 10 minutes at high pressure. Allow to cook.

4. When the cooking is done, release the pressure naturally for 10 minutes and do a quick release.

5. Open the lid and garnish.

Coconut Chicken Curry

Overall cooking time: 45 min

Serving: 46

Nutrition info: Calories: 156, Fat: 4.5g, Carbs: 2g, Protein: 26g.

Ingredients:

Chicken	2.5 lbs.
Cumin seeds	1 Tbsp.
Cardamom	2
Garlic	4 cloves
Tomatoes	5, chopped
Coconut milk	1 can
Salt and pepper	as required

Cooking procedure:

1. Switch the instant pot to sauté and add the oil. When it is hot, add the bay leaves, cloves, cardamom and onion. Sauté for 3 minutes. Then add the tomatoes and sauté for 5 minutes.

2. Then cool the mixture and blend it thoroughly. Add the coconut milk to the blended mixture.

3. Now, go to the sauté function again, add a tablespoon of oil and the cumin seeds. After one minute, add the

chicken and brown it. Then pour in the ground mixture and mix well with the chicken.

4. Secure the lid and manually set the time to 10 minutes at high pressure. Allow to cook.

5. When the cooking is done, release the pressure naturally for 10 minutes and do a quick release.

6. Serve.

Delicious Sweet Potato Chicken

Overall cooking time: 35 min

Serving: 5

Nutrition info: Calories: 304, Fat: 15g, Carbs: 32g, Protein: 5.6g.

Ingredients:

Ghee	2 Tbsp.
Yellow onion	½, diced
Garlic	3 cloves
Chicken breast	1 lb.
Sweet potato	1, cubed
Red pepper	1
Green beans	2 cups
Chicken broth	2/3 cup
Curry powder	3 Tbsp.
Cumin	1 Tbsp.
Turmeric	1 tsp.
Cayenne	½ tsp.
Sea salt	½ tsp.
Coconut milk	14 oz.

Cooking procedure:

1. Set the instant pot to sauté temperature and add the ghee to it. When heated, add the onion and garlic and sauté for 3 minutes.

2. Now, add the sweet potato, chicken, green beans, red pepper, curry, broth, turmeric, cumin, salt and cayenne. Secure the lid and manually set the time to 10 minutes at high pressure. Allow to cook.

3. When the cooking is done, release the pressure naturally for 10 minutes and do a quick release.

4. Open the lid and turn back to sauté function and stir in coconut milk.

5. Serve with cauliflower rice.

Tasty Chicken with Vegetables

Overall cooking time: 50 min

Serving: 6

Nutrition info: Calories: 239, Fat: 11g, Carbs: 23g, Protein: 12g.

Ingredients:

chicken chuck roast	½ lbs.
Salt and pepper	½ Tbsp.
Olive oil	2 Tbsp.
Onion	1, chopped
Garlic cloves	4, minced
chicken broth	¾ cup
Soy sauce	½ cup

Brown sugar cup	1/3
Sesame oil	2 Tbsp.
Red pepper	1/8 tsp.
Broccoli florets	1 lb.
Water	3 Tbsp.
Cornstarch	3 Tbsp.

Cooking procedure:

1. Heat your instant pot to sauté temperature and add the olive oil into the hot pan. Season chicken with pepper and salt. Set aside.

2. Add the onion to the pot and sauté for 2 minutes. Add the garlic and sauté for 1 minute.

3. Now add red pepper, sesame oil, brown sugar, soy sauce and chicken broth and stir until the sugar dissolves.

4. Add the chicken and close the lid. Set the time for 12 minutes at high pressure.

5. Meanwhile put the broccoli into a microwave with ¼ cup water and cook until tender.

6. In a mixing cup, mix the cornstarch with water and add to the instant pot and add the broccoli too. Cook for 5 minutes more without the lid or until you like.

Delicious Chicken Biryani

Overall cooking time: 27 min

Serving: 2

Nutrition info: Calories: 237, Fat: 8g, Carbs: 22g, Protein: 18g.

Ingredients:

For chicken

Chicken thighs	300gm	Onion	1
Ground cumin	1 Tbsp.	Bay leaf	1
Garam masala	1 Tbsp.	Ginger	1 inch
Chili powder	½ Tbsp.	Garlic	3
Methi leaves	1 tsp.	cloves	
Lemon juice	2 Tbsp.	Biryani masala	2 tsp.
		Coriander	2 Tbsp.
For the rice		Mint	1 Tbsp.
Cashews	2 Tbsp.	Salt	½ Tbsp.
Butter	1 Tbsp.		

Cooking procedure:

1. First mix the marinade ingredients in a mixing bowl and chill overnight.

2. Go to the sauté function in your instant pot and toast the cashew nuts until brown. Set aside.

3. Now, add the butter and oil, when the butter is fully melted add the bay leaf and onion. Brown the onion. Add

the ginger and garlic and sauté for 1 minute more. Here, add the chicken with marinade ingredients and cook fully. Stir occasionally.

4. Sprinkle in the biryani masala and then pour the rice. Add ½ cup of water and sprinkle the salt. Secure the lid and manually set the time to 10 minutes at high pressure. Allow to cook.

5. When the cooking is done, release the pressure naturally for 10 minutes and do a quick release. Done.

Special Chicken Roast

Overall cooking time: 35 min

Serving: 4

Nutrition info: Calories: 547, Fat: 46g, Carbs: 11g, Protein: 125g.

Ingredients:

Chicken	2 lbs.
Vegetable oil	1 Tbsp.
Garlic	4 cloves
Soy sauce	½ cup
Water	½ cup
Brown sugar	2/3 cup
Ginger	½ tsp., minced
Cornstarch	2 Tbsp.
Onion	3, chopped

Cooking procedure:

1. Set the instant pot to sauté and season chicken with pepper and salt. Set aside.
2. Add the garlic and sauté for 1 minute then add the soy sauce, ginger, brown sugar and ½ cup water. Stir to mix properly.
3. Now add the browned beef and the juices. Turn the instant pot to high pressure and set the time to 12 minutes.
4. Release the pressure and open the lid. Add the cornstarch and 3 Tbsp. of water. Stir continuously and bring the temperature to a boil. Thicken until you're satisfied.

Delicious Capital Chicken

Overall cooking time: 15 min

Serving: 4

Nutrition info: Calories: 400, Fat: 15g, Carbs: 36g, Protein: 38g.

Ingredients:

Olive oil	1 Tbsp.
Onion	1 cup, diced
Bell pepper	1
Minced ginger	1 Tbsp.
Tomato paste	2 Tbsp.
Curry powder	1-2 Tbsp.
Thyme	1 Tbsp.
Sweet paprika	1 Tbsp.
Cayenne pepper	¼ Tbsp.
Mano chutney	½ cup
Chicken broth	½ cup
Chicken thighs	6
Salt and pepper	to taste.

Cooking procedure:

1. Set the instant pot to sauté temperature and add vegetable oil to it. When heated, add the onion and bell pepper and sauté for 2 minutes. Then, add the garlic, curry powder, tomato paste, thyme, cayenne and thyme. Sauté for 2 minutes more.
2. Now add the tomatoes, chicken broth and chutney.
3. Secure the lid and manually set the time to 10 minutes at high pressure. Allow to cook.

4. When the cooking is done, release the pressure naturally for 10 minutes and do a quick release. Serve.

Vegan Butter Chicken

Overall cooking time: 45 min

Serving: 4

Nutrition info: Calories: 134, Fat: 6g, Carbs: 14g, Protein: 7g.

Ingredients:

Rib tomato	3
Garlic	4 cloves
Ginger	½ inch
Green chili	1
Water	¾ cup
Garam masala	1 Tbsp.
Paprika	½ Tbsp.
Cayenne	¼ tsp.
Salt	¾ tsp.
Soy curls	1 cup
Chickpeas	1 cup, cooked
Garam masala	½ tsp.
Sugar	½ Tbsp.
Methi	1 Tbsp.
Hot green chili	½
Ginger	½ Tbsp.

Cooking procedure:

1. Add the chili, tomatoes, ginger and garlic to a blender and blend until smooth.

2. Add the mixture to the instant pot. Add the salt, spices, chickpeas and soy curls. Secure the lid and manually set the time to 10 minutes at high pressure. Allow to cook.

3. When the cooking is done, release the pressure naturally for 10 minutes and do a quick release.

4. Open the lid and turn on the sauté function. Add the garam masala, cashew cream, and sugar, then mix well. Bring to a boil and it's done.

Healthy Chicken Soup

Overall cooking time: 40 min

Serving: 4

Nutrition info: Calories: 232, Fat: 10g, Carbs: 8g, Protein: 20g.

Ingredients:

Chicken	3 lbs.
Carrots	2, chopped
Celery stalk	1
Turnip	¼
Indian seasoning	1 Tbsp.
Bay leaves	2
Garlic	3 cloves
Onion	1, sliced
Sea salt	1 Tbsp.
Black pepper	1 Tbsp.

Cooking procedure:

1. Add the vegetables to the instant pot, then add the chicken and herbs, then pour in 4 cups of water.
2. Close the lid and press the soup function of the instant pot.
3. Release the pressure naturally. Then open the lid and debone the meat.
4. Place the meat in the pot again. Stir to combine with other ingredients. Add the crushed carrots and adjust the salt and pepper if required.

Beef Recipes

Simple Beef Roast

Overall cooking time: 25 min

Serving: 4

Nutrition info: Calories: 190, Fat: 2g, Carbs: 28g, Protein: 6g.

Ingredients:

Beef	1 lb.
Garlic	1 cloves
Soy sauce	¼ cup
olive oil	2 Tbsp.
Ground ginger	¼ tsp.
Garlic	¼ tsp.
Red pepper	¼ tsp.
Cooked rice	2 cups
Onion	3, sliced

Cooking procedure:

1. First, season the beef with all the ingredients except the oil and onion for 2-3 hours.

2. Turn on your instant pot and set to sauté. Add the oil and heat. Add the meat and sauté for 5 minutes.

3. Now close the lid and manually set the time for 15 minutes at high pressure.

4. Transfer the meat to natural depressurization.

Healthy Beef Curry

Overall cooking time: 55 minutes.

Serving: 6

Nutrition info: Calories: 284, Fat: 9g, Carbs: 32g, Protein: 15g.

Ingredients:

Beef chuck	2 lbs.	Jalapeno	1
Vegetable oil	1 Tbsp.	Black pepper	1 tsp.
Salt	to taste	Turmeric powder	1 Tbsp.
Black pepper	for seasoning	Beef broth	2 cups
Onion	1 cup, chopped	Carrots	1 ½ cups
Garlic	5 Tbsp., minced	Potatoes	1 ½ cups
Ginger	1 Tbsp.	Cilantro	½ cup

Cooking procedure:

1. Season the meat with salt and pepper and set aside.

2. Set the instant pot to sauté and add the oil into it. When the oil is heated, add the meat and brown both sides. Remove the meat from the pot.

3. Now add the onion, garlic, jalapenos, ginger and stir well. Brown with 2 Tbsp. of broth.

4. Here, add the beef, pepper, turmeric and sauté the beef until the ingredients make a coating on the beef's surface.

5. Secure the lid and manually set the time to 15 minutes at high pressure. Allow to cook.

6. When the cooking is done, release the pressure naturally for 10 minutes and do a quick release.

7. Open the lid and add the potatoes and carrots. Open the lid and cook for 5 minutes manually.

8. Then go back to the sauté function and add coconut milk. Sauté until thickened.

Beef Stew

Overall cooking time: 60 minutes.
Serving: 6
Nutrition info: Calories: 450, Fat: 27g, Carbs: 40g, Protein: 65g.

Ingredients:

Vegetable oil	3 Tbsp.	Ginger	1 Tbsp.
Beef stew	2 lbs.	Jalapeno	1
Salt and pepper	to taste	Black pepper	1 tsp.
Onion	1 cup, chopped	Turmeric powder	1 Tbsp.
Garlic	5 cloves	A-1 steak sauce	2 Tbsp.
Carrot	2 cups, chopped	Beef broth	2 cups
Potatoes	2 cups, cubed		
Coconut milk	2 cups.		

Cooking procedure:

1. Season the meat with salt, pepper, and garlic on all sides.

2. Press sauté, add the oil, onions, ginger, jalapeno, garlic and stir well.

3. Add 2 Tbsp. of broth and sauté for 4 minutes. Now add the beef, turmeric, black pepper, sauce and stir to coat the beef.

4. Add the broth. Secure the lid and manually set the time to 15 minutes at high pressure. Allow to cook.

5. When the cooking is done do a quick release.

6. Open the lid and add the potatoes and carrots to the instant pot. Close the lid and cook manually for 5 minutes more.

7. Now add the coconut milk and stir to mix properly. Heat it thoroughly using the sauté function.

8. Serve with your love.

Mouthwatering Beef Kheema

Overall cooking time: 25 min

Serving: 4

Nutrition info: Calories: 364, Fat: 21g, Carbs: 18g, Protein: 25g.

Ingredients:

Vegetable oil	1 Tbsp.
Frozen peas	1 cup
Onion	1 cup, chopped
Minced ginger	1 Tbsp.
Garlic	1 Tbsp.
Cinnamon sticks	3 pieces
Cardamom	4 pods
Ground beef	1 lb.
Garam masala	1 Tbsp.
Salt	1 tsp.
Turmeric	½ Tbsp.
Cayenne pepper	½ tsp.
Coriander	1 ½ tsp.
Cumin	½ tsp.
Water	¼ cup

Cooking procedure:

1. Go to the sauté function on your instant pot and add the oil first. Then add the cinnamon sticks and the cardamom. Sizzle for 40 seconds.
2. Add the onion, ginger and garlic and sauté for 3 minutes.
3. Now add the beef and sauté a little for 5 minutes. Add the spices and the water. Secure the lid and manually set the time to 10 minutes at high pressure. Allow to cook.
4. When the cooking is done, release the pressure naturally for 10 minutes and do a quick release.
5. Open the lid and add the peas. Heat for 5-10 minutes in sauté function.

Delicious Beef Masala

Overall cooking time: 40 min
Serving: 4
Nutrition info: Calories: 210, Fat: 12g, Carbs: 3g, Protein: 22g.

Ingredients:

Stewing beef	2 lbs.
Onion	2, chopped
Garlic	3 cloves
Tomato	½ cup, crushed
Cilantro	¼ cup
Salt and pepper	to taste
Turmeric	1 tsp.
Garam masala	1 Tbsp.
Cumin	½ tsp.
Coriander	½ tsp.
Cayenne pepper	½ tsp.
Paprika	½ tsp.
Lemon zest	½ Tbsp.
Oli	1 Tbsp.
Beef stock	½ cup

Cooking procedure:

1. Go to the sauté function; add the onion, garlic, oil, salt and pepper, and the ginger and sauté for 3 minutes.
2. Add the crushed tomatoes, and sugar and heat to boiling. Place the mixture in a blender and blend until smooth.

3. Add the meat to the instant pot and brown on both sides. Add the blended mixture and the other ingredients. Secure the lid and manually set the time to 30 minutes at high pressure. Allow to cook.
4. When the cooking is done, release the pressure naturally for 10 minutes and do a quick release.
5. Serve when tender.

Healthy Goat Curry

Overall cooking time: 52 minutes.

Serving: 4

Nutrition info: Calories: 284, Fat: 9g, Carbs: 32g, Protein: 15g.

Ingredients:

goat chuck	1.5 lbs.
Vegetable oil	1 Tbsp.
Salt	to taste
Black pepper	for seasoning
Onion	½ cup, chopped
Garlic	3 Tbsp., minced
Ginger	1 Tbsp.
Jalapeno	1
Black pepper	1 tsp.
Turmeric powder	1 Tbsp.
meat broth	1.5 cups
Carrots	½ cups
Potatoes	½ cups
Cilantro	½ cup

Cooking procedure:

1. Season the meat with salt and pepper and set aside.

2. Set the instant pot to sauté and add the oil to it. When the oil is heated, add the meat and brown both sides. Remove the meat from the pot.

3. Now add the onion, garlic, jalapenos, ginger and stir well. Brown with 2 Tbsp. of broth.
4. Here, add the beef, pepper, and turmeric then sauté the meat until the ingredients make a coating on the beef's surface.
5. Secure the lid and manually set the time to 15 minutes at high pressure. Allow to cook.
6. When the cooking is done, release the pressure naturally for 10 minutes and do a quick release.
7. Open the lid and add the potatoes and carrots. Close the lid and cook for 5 minutes manually.
8. Then go back to the sauté function and add the coconut milk. Sauté until thickened.

Beef Vindaloo

Overall cooking time: 50 min

Serving: 2

Nutrition info: Calories: 268, Fat: 10g, Carbs: 28g, Protein: 22g.

Ingredients:

Beef shin.	1lb.
Onion	1 cup, chopped
Chili	2
Tomato	2, chopped
Ghee	2 Tbsp.

For the marinade:

Cinnamon	½ Tbsp.
Ground cloves	¼ Tbsp.
Mango powder	1 Tbsp.
Turmeric	1 Tbsp.
Cumin	½ Tbsp.
Chili powder	2 Tbsp.
Pepper	½ Tbsp.
Onion	50gm
Garlic	8 cloves
Ginger	25gm
Lemon juice	1 Tbsp.
Honey	1 Tbsp.
Tamarind pulp	50ml
Cardamom pods	12

Cooking procedure:

1. First, add all the marinade ingredients, except the pods, to a blender and blend until smooth. Now, in a large bowl, add the mixture with the chopped beef and allow to marinate for 12 hours. Add the pods too.

2. Turn on the sauté function and sauté the onion for 5 minutes. Then add the beef and marinade ingredients. Sauté for another 5 minutes.

3. Now add the other ingredients. Secure the lid and manually set the cooking time to 35 minutes at high pressure. Allow to cook. When it is done, allow 10 minutes natural release and then do a quick release.

4. Open the lid and turn the cooker back to the sauté function and sauté to thicken for around 10 minutes.

Delicious Beef Dopiaza

Overall cooking time: 60 min

Serving: 2

Nutrition info: Calories: 753, Fat: 49g, Carbs: 24g, Protein: 55g.

Ingredients:

Onion	1 ½ cups
Garlic	6 cloves
Ginger	50gm
Chili pepper	3
Ghee	2 Tbsp.
Cardamom pods	3
Chili powder	1 tsp.
Coriander	1 Tbsp.
Cumin	2 Tbsp.
Turmeric	1 Tbsp.
Beef shin.	1 lb.
Fenugreek leaf	1 Tbsp.
Tomato paste	2 Tbsp.
Dark brown sugar	1 tsp.
Salt	1 tsp.
Garam masala	1 Tbsp.

Cooking procedure:

1. First, add the one-third of the onion with garlic and ginger to a blender and blend to paste consistency.

2. Turn on the sauté function and add the other two-thirds of the onion with 1 Tbsp of ghee and sauté for 3 minutes. Set aside.

3. Now, add the rest of the ghee to the instant pot with the garlic-onion paste and sauté for 2 minutes. Add the cardamom pods, cumin, turmeric and chili powders. Stir for 30 seconds.

4. Add the meat and stir to coat. Add the other ingredients. Secure the lid and manually set the cooking time to 25 minutes at high pressure. Allow to cook.

5. When it is done, allow 10 minutes natural release and then do a quick release.

6. Separate the meat from the instant pot and sauté the sauce for 20-30 min. Place back the meat in the instant pot, add the fried onion and bring the temperature up before serving.

Kerala Beef Fry

Overall cooking time: 55 min

Serving:

Nutrition info: Calories: 320, Fat: 11g, Carbs: 1g, Protein: 50g.

Ingredients:

Coconut oil	3 Tbsp.
Black mustard seeds	1 Tbsp.
Onion	1, sliced
Serrano pepper	2
Curry leaves	35-40
Ginger	1/4, chopped
Garlic	¼ cup
Spice mix	5 Tbsp.
Beef stew	2 lbs.
Coconut sliced	½ cup.
Lemon juice	2 Tbsp.

Cooking procedure:

1. Set the instant pot to sauté temperature and add the oil into it. When heated, add the mustard seeds to the pot, stir for 30 seconds and then add the onion, curry leaves and serrano peppers. Stir until the onion browns.

2. Now add the spices, other ingredients, garlic and ginger. After 30 seconds, add the beef along with coconut slices. Stir to brown. Add the lemon juice.

3. Secure the lid and manually set the cooking time to 35 minutes at high pressure. Allow to cook.

4. When it is done, allow 10 minutes natural release and then do a quick release.

5. Sauté for 15 minutes to thicken to your desired level.

Lamb Recipes

Kashmiri Lamb Curry

Overall cooking time: 50 min
Serving: 5-6
Nutrition info: Calories: 335, Fat: 22g, Carbs: 0.5g, Protein: 28g.
Ingredients:

Ghee	1 Tbsp.
Diced tomatoes	14 oz.
Lamb stew	1 ½ lbs.
Garlic	4 cloves
Ginger	1-inch piece
Coconut milk	½ cup
Lime juice	½ lime
Sea salt	¼ tsp.
Black pepper	1 pinch
Turmeric	¾ tsp.
Onion	1, diced
Carrots	3, sliced
Zucchini	1, diced
Cilantro	chopped

Cooking procedure:

1. Take a large mixing bowl; mix the meat with garlic, ginger, lime, milk, pepper and salt. Transfer the entire mixture to a refrigerator and marinate overnight.
2. Now, transfer the marinated meat to the instant pot and add the tomatoes, ghee, masala, carrots and onions. Seal the lid and manually set the time to 15 minutes at high pressure.
3. Naturally release the pressure and set to sauté. Add the zucchini and cook for 5 to 6 minutes to permit the zucchini to become tender.

4. Garnish with cilantro and serve.

Kacchi Lamb dum Biryani

Overall cooking time: 35 min

Serving: 6

Nutrition info: Calories: 241, Fat: 4g, Carbs: 30g, Protein: 18g.

Ingredients:

Lamb cubes	1 lb.
Greek yogurt	½ cup
Onion	½ cup
Cilantro	½ cup
Mint	¼ cup, chopped
Ginger	1 Tbsp., minced
Garlic	1 Tbsp. minced
Garam masala	2 Tbsp.
Salt	1 Tbsp.
Turmeric	1 Tbsp.
Cayenne pepper	½ Tbsp.
Ground cardamom	¼ tsp.
Rice	1 cup

Cooking procedure:

1. Add the marinade ingredients into a large mixing bowl. Mix well and add the meat. Combine well and marinate for 30 minutes.
2. Place the marinated lamb in the instant pot as well as the marinade ingredients, spices and yogurt; spread the rice over the meat.

3. Pour one cup of water in and then close the lid and manually set the time 6 minutes at high pressure.
4. Naturally release the pressure.
5. Open and garnish with cilantro.

Goat Curry in a Hurry

Overall cooking time: 25 min

Serving: 2

Nutrition info: Calories: 350, Fat: 4.7g, Carbs: 61g, Protein: 17g.

Ingredients:

Olive oil	2 Tbsp.
Goat meat	2 lbs.
Onion	2, diced
Ginger	1 ½ inch
Garlic	3 cloves, minced
Salt and pepper	to taste
Spices	5-6 Tbsp.
Garam masala	1 Tbsp.
Tomato	28 oz.
Water	½ cup
Potato	½ lb.

Cooking procedure:

1. Sauté the meat with olive oil first. Then add the onion, ginger, garlic, spices and the masala. Sauté for 2-3 minutes.

2. Add the potato, tomatoes and water. Fasten the lid and manually set the time to 45 minutes at high pressure. Allow to cook.

3. When the cooking is done, naturally release the pressure for 10 minutes and do a quick release.

4. Open the lid and sauté until thickened.

Kashmiri Curry with Yogurt

Overall cooking time: 40 min

Serving: 5-6

Nutrition info: Calories: 383, Fat: 29g, Carbs: 11g, Protein: 21g.

Ingredients:

Leg of lamb	1 ½ lbs.
Greek yogurt	4 Tbsp.
Masala	½ Tbsp.
Olive oil	1 Tbsp.
Bay leaves	2
Cardamom pods	3
Cinnamon bark	2-inch
Whole cloves	2
Cumin seeds	1 ½ Tbsp.
Fennel seeds	1 Tbsp.
Garlic	2 cloves
Garam masala	½ Tbsp.
Ground chili	½ Tbsp.
Coriander	1 Tbsp.
Ginger	1 Tbsp.
Tomatoes	2
Coriander	1 Tbsp.
Salt and pepper	to taste.

Cooking procedure:

1. In a mixing bowl, mix the lamb with the garam masala and yogurt. Marinate the mixture in the refrigerator for 24 hours.

2. Now, set the instant pot to sauté and add the oil first. After 2 minutes add the spice items except for the powder ingredients and sauté for 3 minutes. Add the garlic and remaining powder ingredients. Near the end of the sautéing, add the tomato and a cup of water.

3. Then add the marinated lamb and stir evenly. Cover the lid and manually set the time to 10 minutes.

4. Remove the lid and turn back to sauté. Stir and cook to your desired tenderness. Add a little salt and pepper if needed.

5. Cook rice on your stove to serve together.

Easiest Mutton Curry

Overall cooking time: 55 min
Serving: 7
Nutrition info: Calories: 292, Fat: 19g, Carbs: 1g, Protein: 29g.

Ingredients:

Olive oil	3 Tbsp.
Bay leaf	1
Cinnamon stick	1
Cardamom pods	4
Cloves	4
Green chili	1
Onion	3, chopped
Ginger-garlic paste	1 Tbsp.
Tomatoes	4, chopped
Coriander powder	1 Tbsp.
Mutton masala	2 Tbsp.
Mutton	1lb.
Potatoes	2, quartered
Garam masala	1 tsp.
Kasuri methi	1 tsp.
Ghee	1 Tbsp.
Salt and pepper	to taste

Cooking procedure:

1. Go to the sauté function and add the bay leaf, cloves, cardamom and cinnamon and sauté for 1 minute. Then add the garlic paste, onion and chili, and cook for 6 to 7 minutes until translucent.

2. Now add the mutton masala, coriander powder and the tomatoes to the instant pot and cook for 6 minutes. Then add the salt, potatoes, mutton, and water. Fasten the lid and manually set the time to 35 minutes at high pressure. Allow to cook.

3. When the cooking is done, naturally release the pressure for 10 minutes and do a quick release.

4. Open the lid and turn back to the sauté function and add a little water if it is too thick. Add the garam masala, and ghee and simmer for 5 minutes.

Vegetables Recipes

Potato Salad

Overall cooking time: 45 min

Serving: 5-6

Nutrition info: Calories: 357, Fat: 20g, Carbs: 27g, Protein: 8g.

Ingredients:
Potato   6, scrubbed
Water   1 cup
Onion   1 cup, chopped
Celery   1, chopped
Cooked egg   3
Dill   1 Tbsp.
Mustard   1 Tbsp.
Cider vinegar 1 Tbsp.
Salt and pepper to taste

Cooking procedure:

1. Take the instant pot and add the potatoes, then pour in the water. Fasten the lid and manually set the time to 5 minutes at high pressure. Allow to cook.
2. When the cooking is done, naturally release the pressure and take the potatoes, peel and dice.
3. In a mixing bowl, combine the onion, celery, dill, salt and pepper and mix with the diced potatoes.
4. Then mix with mustard, vinegar and mayonnaise. Chill before serving.

Homemade Mashed Potatoes

Overall cooking time: 30 min

Serving: 4

Nutrition info: Calories: 107, Fat: 5g, Carbs: 17g, Protein: 2g.

Ingredients:

Potatoes	2 lbs.
Garlic	6 cloves
Chicken stock	2/3 cup
Salt	¾ Tbsp.
Butter	3 Tbsp.
Sour cream	¼ cup
Cheese	¼ cup

Cooking Procedure:

1. Add the potatoes, salt, half of the butter, garlic and water to the instant pot. Fasten the lid and manually set the time to 8 minutes at high pressure. Allow to cook.

2. When the cooking is done, do a quick release.

3. Open the lid and mash the potatoes to smooth. Add the remaining butter, cream cheese and the sour cream. Sauté a little.

Healthy Crispy Potatoes

Overall cooking time: 15 min

Serving: 4

Nutrition info: Calories: 125 Fat: 4g, Carbs: 23g, Protein: 3g.

Ingredients:

Yukon gold potatoes	1 lb.
Olive oil	1 Tbsp.
Salt and pepper	to taste
Turmeric powder	¼ Tbsp.
Chili powder	¼ Tbsp.
Black vinegar	2 Tbsp.

Cooking procedure:

1. Add the potatoes to the instant pot. Add ½ cup of water. Fasten the lid and manually set the time to 5 minutes at high pressure. Allow to cook.

2. When the cooking is done, naturally release the pressure for 10 minutes and do a quick release.

3. Open the lid and turn on the sauté function. Add the olive oil and other ingredients. Cook until the surface of the potatoes becomes crispy.

Delicious Chickpea Curry

Overall cooking time: 35 min
Serving: 6
Nutrition info: Calories: 384, Fat: 8g,
Carbs: 68g, Protein: 11g.

Ingredients:

Olive oil	2 Tbsp.
Onion	1
Garlic	4 cloves
Salt	1 Tbsp.
pepper	1 Tbsp.
cumin	1 Tbsp.
turmeric	1 Tbsp.
cinnamon	1 Tbsp.
Chili flakes	½ Tbsp.
Chickpeas	15 oz.
Chickpeas	3 cups
Tomato	400gm
Potato	3 large, cubed
Water	½ cup

Cooking Procedure:

1. First sauté the cumin seeds in olive oil for 30 seconds and then add the onion and stir for 5 minutes.
2. Then add the garlic and all other ingredients. Fasten the lid and manually set the time to 15 minutes at high pressure. Allow to cook.
3. When the cooking is done, naturally release the pressure for 10 minutes and do a quick release.

4. Open the lid and sprinkle parsley before serving.

Easy Boiled Potatoes

Overall cooking time: 15 min

Serving: 2-3

Nutrition info: Calories: 87, Fat: 0g, Carbs: 20.5g, Protein: 2g.

Ingredients:

Potatoes	2 lbs.
Water	1 liter

Cooking procedure:

1. In an instant pot, add the potatoes and pour in the water. Fasten the lid and manually set the time to 10 minutes at high pressure. Allow to cook.

2. When the cooking is done, do a quick release.

3. Open the lid and you have boiled potatoes. You can eat them with sauce and salt or serve with other dishes.

Aloo Gobi Cauliflower

Overall cooking time: 20 min

Serving: 4

Nutrition info: Calories: 161, Fat: 14g, Carbs: 8g, Protein: 4g.

Ingredients:

Cauliflower	1 medium
Olive oil	2 Tbsp.
Salt	¼ Tbsp.
Parsley	½ tsp.
Seasoning	1 Tbsp.
Cilantro	as required
Lime juice	½ Tbsp.

Cooking procedure:

1. In the instant pot, add the cauliflower pieces and a cup of water. Close the lid. Manually set the time for 2 minutes. It will take 10 minutes to develop the pressure.

2. When it is done, remove the cauliflower and set aside.

3. If there is any extra water, remove from the pot and bring the cooker to sauté. Add the oil and then add the cauliflower. Break up the flower with the help of a potato masher.

4. Add the spices and ingredients with salt and pepper.

5. Serve with sauces or with other dishes.

Aloo Gobi Potatoes

Overall cooking time: 20 min

Serving: 6

Nutrition info: Calories: 84, Fat: 1.9g, Carbs: 12g, Protein: 3g.

Ingredients:

Olive oil	1 Tbsp.
Cumin seeds	1 Tbsp.
Cauliflower	1 medium
Potatoes	2 cups, sliced
Tomato	½ cup
Salt and pepper	to taste
Garam masala	1 Tbsp.
Turmeric	½ tsp.
Cumin	¼ Tbsp.
Coriander	½ Tbsp.
Water	¼ cup

Cooking procedure:

1. Sauté the cumin seeds in olive oil for 1 minute from the start and then add the potatoes and sauté until brown.

2. Now add the spices and sauté for 2 minutes more. Add the water, tomatoes and the cauliflower. Close the lid and manually set the time for 2 minutes at low pressure.

3. Do a quick release and garnish with cilantro.

Healthy Potato Shaak

Overall cooking time: 15 min

Serving: 2

Nutrition info: Calories: 141, Fat: 3g, Carbs: 22g, Protein: 2g.

Ingredients:

Vegetable oil	1 Tbsp.
Cumin seeds	1 tsp.
Mustard seeds	1 tsp.
Red chili	1
Curry leaves	a few
Potatoes	1lb.
Onion	1, sliced
Water	¾ cup
Salt and pepper	to taste
Turmeric powder	1 tsp.

Cooking procedure:

1. Go to the sauté function on your instant pot and add the oil. When heated, add the mustard seeds and stir until they start popping. Then add the red chili, curry leaves and cumin seeds. Toast the ingredients.

2. Now add the potatoes, turmeric, pepper powder, water and onion. Close the lid and manually set the time for 10 minutes.

3. Done.

Aloo Baingan Masala

Overall cooking time: 24 min

Serving: 5

Nutrition info: Calories: 97, Fat: 12g, Carbs: 21g, Protein: 3g.

Ingredients:

Cooking oil	2 ½ Tbsp.
Onion	1 cup, sliced
Bell pepper	1 cup
Green chili	1, chopped
Garlic	5 cloves
Ginger	1 inch, grated
Tomatoes	4, puree
Cashews	6, soaked
Eggplants	8
Potato	3, quartered
Water	½ cup
Cumin	1 Tbsp.
Turmeric powder	1 Tbsp.
Garam masala	1 Tbsp.
Chili powder	2 Tbsp.
Salt	to taste

Cooking procedure:

1. Combine the tomatoes and cashews together and grind well. Set aside.

2. Set the instant pot to sauté and add the oil. Add the onion and sauté for 30 seconds and then add the garlic,

ginger, green chilies, masala and bell pepper. Mix well with continuous stirring.

3. Add the water and tomato puree. Do not stir. Add the potatoes and the eggplant at the top. Close the lid and manually set the time for 3 minutes.

4. Naturally release the pressure. Stir to mix all. Adjust the seasoning.

Healthy Garlic Mashed Potatoes

Overall cooking time: 20 min

Serving: 8

Nutrition info: Calories: 86, Fat: 0g, Carbs: 20g, Protein: 2g.

Ingredients:

Water	1 cup
Potatoes	3 lbs.
Garlic	4 cloves
Milk	¾ cup
Butter	3 Tbsp.
Kosher salt	1.5 Tbsp.
Black pepper	½ Tbsp.
Parsley	for garnish

Cooking procedure:

1. Place the potatoes and garlic with sufficient water in an instant pot and close the lid. Manually set the time for 5 minutes at high pressure.

2. Open the lid and drain excess water from the pot. Mash the potatoes until smooth.

3. Add the other ingredients and mix well.

Simple Spinach Dal

Overall cooking time: 25 min

Serving: 4

Nutrition info: Calories: 110, Fat: 5g, Carbs: 13g, Protein: 5.

Ingredients:

Ghee	2 Tbsp.
Cumin seeds	1 Tbsp.
Turmeric	¼ Tbsp.
Chilies	2
Garlic	2 Tbsp.
Curry leaves	8
Lentils	1 cup
Spinach	2 cups, chopped
Salt	2 Tbsp.
Water	4 cups

Cooking procedure:

1. Turn on the sauté function and add the ghee. When the ghee is hot, add the cumin seeds and sauté for 30 seconds. Add the curry leaves, chilies and garlic. Mix.
2. Now add the tomatoes, lentils and salt. Add 2 cups of water and close the lid. Manually set the time for 15 minutes at high pressure.
3. Naturally release the pressure and then add desired amount of water to get desired consistency.
4. Blend the lentils and add the spinach. Mix thoroughly. Bring the daal to boiling and season.

Easy Mukh Daal

Overall cooking time: 20 min

Serving: 5-6

Nutrition info: Calories: 121, Fat: 2g, Carbs: 22g, Protein: 4g.

Ingredients:

Mukh daal	1 cup
Garlic	1 Tbsp.
Ginger	1 Tbsp.
Salt	to taste
Pepper	1, chopped
Olive oil	1 Tbsp.
Garam masala	½ Tbsp.

Cooking procedure:

1. Combine the daal and 2 cups of water to the instant pot and close the lid. Manually set the time for 15 minutes at high pressure.

2. Release the pressure naturally and then mash the daal and add the garlic and ginger paste. Add the all other ingredients and sauté for 5 minutes to heat the daal through.

3. Serve with rice.

Delicious Palak Paneer

Overall cooking time: 15 min

Serving: 4

Nutrition info: Calories: 300, Fat: 11g, Carbs: 35g, Protein: 12g.

Ingredients:

Spinach	1 lb. Paneer	2 cups, cubed
Ghee	2 Tbsp.	
Cumin	1 Tbsp.	
Onion	1, chopped	
Green chili	2 Tbsp.	
Garlic	1 Tbsp.	
Ginger	1 Tbsp.	
Cashews	15	
Milk	4 Tbsp.	
Garam masala	1 Tbsp.	
Salt	to taste	

Cooking procedure:

1. First add the cashews to milk and blend to a paste. Set aside.
2. Go to the sauté function on your instant pot and add the ghee. When it is hot, add the green chilies, ginger, garlic and cumin seeds. Sauté for one minute. Then add the onion and stir for 3 minutes.
3. Then add the spinach and close the lid. Manually set the time to 1 minute at high pressure. Do a quick release.

4. Now, using an immersion blender blend the ingredients well. Add the cashew paste, paneer and the garam masala. Stir to mix and serve.

Delicious Carrot Halwa

Overall cooking time: 30 min

Serving: 6

Nutrition info: Calories: 185, Fat: 5g, Carbs: 31g, Protein: 5g.

Ingredients:

Ghee	2 Tbsp.
Carrots	10 cups, grated
Almond milk	1 cup
Sugar	¾ cup
Almond meal	1 cup
Cardamom	2 Tbsp. (powder)
Raisins	2 Tbsp.
Saffron	½ Tbsp.
Almonds	2 Tbsp.

Cooking procedure:

1. Go to the sauté function on your instant pot and add the carrots and oil. Sauté for 3 minutes. Add the almond milk and manually set the time to 5 minutes at high pressure. Do not forget to close the lid first.
2. Release the pressure, open the lid and add the almond meal, raisins, sugar, saffron, and cardamom powder. Mix properly.
3. Turn back to sauté function and cook for 5 minutes more.
4. Garnish with pistachios or almonds.

Healthy Lentils and Vegetable Khichdi

Overall cooking time: 40 min

Serving: 6

Nutrition info: Calories: 175, Fat: 2g, Carbs: 34g, Protein: 6g.

Ingredients:

Ghee	2 Tbsp.
Cumin seeds	1 Tbsp.
Ginger	1 Tbsp.
Carrots	1, chopped
Beans	¼ cup
Peas	¼ cup
Potato	1, cubed
Cauliflower	1 cup
Cabbage	1 cup
Spinach	1 cup
Turmeric	½ Tbsp.
Salt and pepper to taste	

Cooking procedure:

1. Add the ghee to the instant pot and turn it to the sauté function. Add the cumin seeds and ginger. Sauté for 30 seconds.

2. Now add the vegetables and stir to mix well.

3. Add the chili powder, salt lentils and turmeric. Mix well. Add 6 cups of water and close the lid. Manually set the time for 12 minutes at high pressure.

4. Once done, release the pressure, open the lid and garnish with cilantro.

5. Serve hot

Mung Bean Dahl

Overall cooking time: 30 min

Serving: 2-4

Nutrition info: Calories: 350, Fat: .4g, Carbs: 52g, Protein: 29g.

Ingredients:

Mung beans	½ cup
Vegetable stock	2 cups
Curry powder	2 Tbsp.
Salt	½ tsp.
Onion powder	½ tsp.
Garlic powder	¼ tsp.
Black pepper	¼ tsp.

Cooking procedure:

1. Add the garlic, onion, salt, curry powder, stock and the mung beans to the instant pot. Close the lid and manually set the time for 25 minutes at high pressure. Allow to cook.

2. Once the cooking is done, do a quick release and then smash with a fork.

3. Add the spinach, stir and cook for 5 minutes more using the sauté function.

Dum Aloo

Overall cooking time: 30 min

Serving: 3

Nutrition info: Calories: 397, Fat: 19g, Carbs: 50g, Protein: 9g.

Ingredients:

Baby potatoes   10
Ghee   2 Tbsp.
Onion   1, chopped
Ginger   2 Tbsp.
Garlic   2 Tbsp.
Tomatoes   2, pureed
Turmeric   ½ Tbsp.
Kashmiri chili   1 Tbsp.
Garam masala   1 Tbsp.
Salt   1 tsp.
Cashews   10

Cooking procedure:

1. First, add the cashews to warm milk. Allow to soak for 10 minutes and set aside.
2. Sauté the onion with ghee for 2 minutes and then add the ginger and garlic. Sauté for 30 seconds and then add the potatoes, turmeric, garam masala, salt, red chili, and tomato paste. Stir to mix all.
3. Add ½ cup of water, close the lid, and manually set the time to 10 minutes at high pressure. Allow to cook.

4. Once the cooking is done, do a quick release. Blend the soaked cashews with milk and add the potatoes. Go to sauté mode again and bring to boil and then turn off.

Side-Dish
Recipes

Bell Pepper and Potato Stir-fry

Overall cooking time: 20 min

Serving: 2

Nutrition info: Calories: 168, Fat: 2g, Carbs: 23g, Protein: 1g.

Ingredients:

Oil	1 Tbsp.
Bell pepper	2
Baby potatoes	4, cut into small pieces
Cumin seeds	½ Tbsp.
Garlic	4 cloves
Dry mango	½ tsp.
Spices	3 ½ Tbsp.

Cooking procedure:

1. Sauté the cumin seeds and garlic together with oil. Then add the bell pepper, spices and potatoes. Stir well.

2. Close the lid and manually set the time for 3 minutes at high pressure. Allow to cook.

3. Once the cooking is done, do a quick release.

4. Add the mango powder and mix.

Delicious Mumbai Pav Bhaji

Overall cooking time: 35 min

Serving: 6

Nutrition info: Calories: 120, Fat: 3g, Carbs: 16g, Protein: 3g.

Ingredients:

Butter	2 Tbsp.
Onion	2, chopped
Garlic	1 inch
Ginger	3 cloves
Red chili	3
Potatoes	4, chopped
Cauliflower	2 cups
Green peas	1 cup
Pav masala	2 Tbsp.
Salt	2 2/3 Tbsp.
Lemon juice	1 Tbsp.
Pav	10
Butter	2 Tbsp.

Cooking procedure:

1. Turn on your instant pot to sauté function and add the butter. When heated add the onion and sauté for 3-4 minutes.
2. Then add the pav, salt, chili, carrots, cauliflower, carrots, green peas and pav bhaji. Stir to mix well.
3. Close the lid and manually set the time for 10 minutes at high pressure. Allow to cook.

4. Once the cooking is done, do a quick release and blend coarsely using an immersion blender.
5. Spread the lemon juice and sauté for a minute.

Simple Aloo Beans

Overall cooking time: 15 min

Serving: 3

Nutrition info: Calories: 143, Fat: 0g, Carbs: 34g, Protein: 5g.

Ingredients:

Oil	1 Tbsp.
Cumin seeds	½ Tbsp.
Garlic	4 cloves
Chili	1, chopped
Green beans	2 cups
Potatoes	1, cut into small pieces
Spices	3 Tbsp.
Mango	1 Tbsp. (powder)
Salt and pepper to taste	

Cooking procedure:

1. Go to the sauté function on your instant pot and add the oil first. When heated, add the cumin seeds, green chili and garlic. Sauté for 2 minutes.
2. Add the green beans, potatoes and spices. Close the lid and manually set the time for 2 minutes at high pressure. Allow to cook.
3. Once the cooking is done, allow the pressure to release naturally. Now add the mango powder. Stir and turn back to sauté function to the desired consistency.
4. Ready for serving.

Kitiri Beans and Vegetables

Overall cooking time: 15 min

Serving: 6

Nutrition info: Calories: 197, Fat: 3g, Carbs: 33g, Protein: 10g.

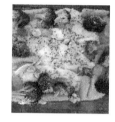

Ingredients:

Split mung beans	1 cup
Basmati rice	1 cup
Frozen vegetables	3 cups
Olive oil	1 Tbsp.
Curry powder	1 Tbsp.
Salt	1 tsp.
Water	8 cups

Cooking procedure:

1. Add the oil, split mung beans, rice and curry powder to the instant pot and press the sauté button.
2. Sauté until coated. Now add the vegetables, water and salt. Close the lid and manually set the time to 8-10 minutes at high pressure.
3. Allow to cook and then release the pressure manually.

Garnish as you like and serve with yogurt and salad.

Vegetables with Lentils

Overall cooking time: 50 min

Serving: 10

Nutrition info: Calories: 48, Fat: 0g, Carbs: 9g, Protein: 3.7g.

Ingredients:

Soy protein	¼ cup
Dried onion	½ cup
Dried lentils	½ cup
Zucchini	1 cup
Diced potato	1
Carrot	1 cup, chopped
Green beans	½ cup
Tomato	½, chopped
Salt	a pinch
Black pepper	¼ Tbsp.
Basil leaves	2
Garlic	2 cloves
Beef bouillon cube	2
Tomato sauce	¼ cup
Water	6 cups

Cooking procedure:

1. Add all the ingredients to the instant pot and cover the lid. Set the time for 15 minutes at high pressure.

2. When it is done, release the pressure naturally and done.

3. It's ready.

Quick and Easy Chana Masala

Overall cooking time: 15 min

Serving: 2

Nutrition info: Calories: 211, Fat: 3.5g, Carbs: 39g, Protein: 9g.

Ingredients:

Chickpeas	1 cup
Onion	1
Tomato	1
Green chili	2
Garlic	4 cloves
Ginger	1 inch
Bay leaves	3
Chili powder	1 Tbsp.
Turmeric powder	1 tsp.
Coriander powder	1 tsp.
Garam masala	1 tsp.
Vegetable oil	2 Tbsp.
Salt and pepper	to taste

Cooking procedure:

1. First soak chickpeas in water for 6 to 8 hours.
2. Place the peas into the instant pot, close the lid, and cook for 10 minutes until tender. Set aside.
3. Now, sauté the onion with oil in the pressure cooker. Add the ginger and garlic paste and sauté for 30 seconds more. Then add the red chili powder, coriander salt, garam masala and turmeric powder. Sauté for 3 minutes.

4. Add the water and other ingredients. Close the lid and set the time for 7 minutes.

Juicing for Health

Overall cooking time: 25 min

Serving: 8

Nutrition info: Calories: 220, Fat: 1.5g, Carbs: 52g, Protein: 4.5.

Ingredients:

Carrots	2 large
Celery stalks	2
Beet	1
Cucumber	1
Apple	1
Parsley	10 sprigs
Snap beans	12

Cooking procedure:

1. Wash the vegetables thoroughly and place in your pressure cooker. Close the lid and cook for 5 minutes at high pressure.

2. Using an immersion blender, blend well.

Easy Vegetarian Quiche

Overall cooking time: 60 min

Serving: 8

Nutrition info: Calories: 160, Fat: 9g, Carbs: 5.5g, Protein: 13g.

Ingredients:

Egg	12
Milk	½ cup
Mushrooms	½ cup
Tomatoes	½ cup
Asparagus spears	12
Spinach	½ cup
Onion	¼ cup
Cayenne pepper	½ Tbsp.
Black pepper	½ Tbsp.
Garlic salt	½ Tbsp.
Cheddar cheese	1 cup

Cooking procedure:

1. Add all the vegetables but tomatoes to the instant pot and close the lid. Manually set the time for 10 minutes at high pressure. Allow to cook until tender.
2. Turn off the cooker and naturally release the pressure. Break the eggs into a blender. Add ½ cup of milk and blend until smooth.
3. Take a casserole dish and grease well. Add and combine all the ingredients in casserole dish and bake for 45 minutes.

Rajma Red Kidney Beans

Overall cooking time: 50 min
Serving: 6
Nutrition info: Calories: 151, Fat: 2g, Carbs: 24g, Protein: 7g.

Ingredients:

Onion Masala:

Olive oil	1 Tbsp.
Onion	1 ½ cup, diced
Minced ginger	1 Tbsp.
Garlic	1 Tbsp.
Diced tomatoes	1 cup
Cayenne pepper	1 Tbsp.
Turmeric	1 Tbsp.
Garam masala	1 Tbsp.
Ground cumin	1 Tbsp.
Salt	1 Tbsp.
Ground coriander	1 Tbsp.
Water	1/3 cup

For kidney beans:

Kidney beans	1 cup
Water	2 cups

Cooking procedure:

1. Place all the ingredients for the onion masala in the inner pot of the instant pot and place the trivet over them.

2. In a heat-proof bowl add the kidney beans and 2 cups of water. Cover with foil. Place on the trivet.

3. Now, secure the lid, press the BEAN button of the instant pot, and cook for 30 minutes.

4. Open the lid and remove the beans and the trivet. Mash the rajma with the back of a spoon.

5. Go to sauté, add the rajma and bring to a boil for 30 min.

Simple Rajma Masala

Overall cooking time: 4 hours and 50 min

Serving: 4

Nutrition info: Calories: 400, Fat: 14g, Carbs: 54g, Protein: 3g.

Ingredients:

Rajma   1 cup
Oil   1 Tbsp.
Cumin seeds   1 Tbsp.
Ginger   1 inch, chopped
Garlic   5 cloves
Green chili   1
Onion   1, chopped
Water   2 cups
Salt   1 tsp.
Rajma masala   2 Tbsp.
Cilantro to garnish.

Cooking procedure:

1. Set the pot to sauté and add the olive oil with green chili, cumin seeds, garlic and ginger. After 30 seconds, add the onion and sauté for 3 minutes.
2. Now add the tomatoes, rajma masala and salt. Sauté for 4-5 minutes. Now add the soaked rajma and the water to the instant pot and press the Bean button. Cook for 30 minutes.
3. Garnish with cilantro and serve.

Palak Ki Khichdi

Overall cooking time: 60 min

Serving: 4

Nutrition info: Calories: 280, Fat: 6g, Carbs: 120g, Protein: 26g.

Ingredients:

Vegetables oil	3 Tbsp.
Cumin seeds	1 Tbsp.
Chili	1
Ginger	1 Tbsp.
Garlic	1 Tbsp.
Tomato	3, chopped
Green spinach	½ lb.
Grain rice	1 cup
Toor daal	1 cup
Turmeric powder	½ tsp.
Salt	to taste

Cooking procedure:

1. Go to the sauté function and add the oil. When heated, add the cumin seeds and after 30 seconds add the garlic and ginger paste. Then add the tomatoes and fry until soft.
2. Now add the spinach, rice, toor daal and salt. Pour in 3 cups of water and set the time for 10 minutes.
3. Open the lid and go to the sauté function. Stir and cook until the water evaporates.

Healthy Masala Dal

Overall cooking time: 35 min

Serving: 4

Nutrition info: Calories: 280, Fat:2g, Carbs: 23g, Protein: 9g.

Ingredients:

Moong daal	2 cups
Asafetida	¼ tsp.
Turmeric powder	1 tsp.
Red chili powder	1 tsp.
Vegetable oil	2 Tbsp.
Onion	1, chopped
Tomatoes	1, chopped
Garlic and ginger	2 Tbsp.
Coriander powder	2 Tbsp.
Sambar masala	1 tsp.
Ghee	2 Tbsp.
Curry leaves	6
Green chili	2, chopped
Salt	to taste

Cooking procedure:

1. Heat the instant pot using the sauté function and add the vegetable oil, then add the garlic, ginger, masala and powder ingredients. Sauté for 1 minute and then add the tomato and onion. Stir and sauté for 5-6 minutes until the tomatoes become soft.

2. Now add the soaked daal and the other ingredients to the instant pot. Close the lid and manually set the time for 10 minutes at high pressure.
3. When the cooker beeps, the daal should be very soft. Take a spoon and mix. The daal will vanish very soon.
4. Add the ghee and garnish with curry leaves.

Tadka Dal

Overall cooking time: 60 min

Serving: 4

Nutrition info: Calories: 149, Fat: 4g, Carbs: 18g, Protein: 7g.

Ingredients:

Tuvar daal	1 cup
Tomato	1, cubed
Garlic and ginger paste	1 Tbsp.
Salt	to taste
Cooking oil	1 Tbsp.
Turmeric powder	½ tsp.
Ghee	3 Tbsp.
Paanch phoran	1 Tbsp.
Curry leaves	10
Green chilies	2

Cooking procedure:

1. Pour the tuvar daal and the tomatoes, garlic, ginger and salt into the instant pot. Add the turmeric powder and 2 cups of water.
2. Close the lid and manually set the time to 10 minutes at high pressure.
3. When it is done, naturally release the pressure and mash everything with the back of a spoon. You should get a soup-like consistency.
4. Add the ghee and heat it. Add the panch phoran, fry with the ghee for a while and then add the asafetida powder. Stir with the ghee. Now add the mixture to the daal.

5. Stir and bring to a simmer.

Vegetable Broth with Yeast Marmite

Overall cooking time: 25 min

Serving: 4

Nutrition info: Calories: 260, Fat: 1g, Carbs: 30g, Protein: 34g.

Ingredients:

Onion   1/4 cup, chopped
French bean   ¼ cup, chopped
Carrot   ¼ cup, chopped
Cabbage   ¼ cup, chopped
Yeast marmite 1 tsp.
Olive oil   2 tsp.
Barley   5 Tbsp.
Salt   to taste

Cooking procedure:

1. Set the instant pot to sauté and then add the oil and onion. Sauté for 1 minute.

2. Add the chopped vegetables and sauté for 2 minutes more.

3. Now add the other ingredients and close the lid. Cook for 5 minutes at high pressure.

4. Release the pressure and serve.

Nourishing Moong Soup

Overall cooking time: 25 min

Serving: 4

Nutrition info: Calories: 80, Fat: 1.4g, Carbs: 11g, Protein: 5g.

Ingredients:

Moong	½ cup
Oil	1 tsp.
Cumin	¼ tsp.
Curry leaves	5
Asafetida	¼ tsp.
Lemon juice	2 Tbsp.

Cooking procedure:

1. Add the moong to the instant pot and pour in 5 cups of water. Close the lid and set the time for 15 minutes. Then allow to release the pressure naturally. Set aside.

2. Now go to the sauté function and add the cumin seeds to the oil. Then add the asafetida, moong and curry leaves to the instant pot. Mix well.

3. Then add the lemon juice and garnish with coriander leaves.

Hariyali Matki Khichdi

Overall cooking time: 15 min

Serving: 4

Nutrition info: Calories: 202, Fat: 5g, Carbs: 25g, Protein: 7g.

Ingredients:

Matki (moath beans)	½ cup
Rice	½ cup
Ghee	1 Tbsp.
Cardamom pods	2
Black peppercorns	4
Laung	2 cloves
Cinnamon	25 mm
Bay leaves	2

A green paste of coriander, chilies, coconut, garlic, ginger, cumin seeds and lemon about   7 Tbsp.

Cooking procedure:

1. Go to the sauté function and add the ghee. When heated, add the cinnamon, cloves, cardamom, bay leaves and peppercorns and sauté for 30 seconds.

2. Then add the green paste and sauté for 1 minute more. Add the matki, rice and 3 cups of water. Mix and close the lid. Manually set the time for 10 minutes at high pressure.

3. Open the lid and serve with garnish.

Mouthwatering Non-fried Kachori

Overall cooking time: 30 min

Serving: 4

Nutrition info: Calories: 183, Fat: 6g, Carbs: 26g, Protein: 5g.

Ingredients:

For the dough:
Plain flour   ¾ cup
Ghee   2 Tbsp.
Salt to taste

For the stuffing:
Oil   2 Tbsp. / Cumin seeds   ½ Tbsp.
Fennel seeds ½ Tbsp.
Asafeotida   ½ tsp.
Turmeric powder   ½ tsp.
Chili powder   ½ tsp.
Ginger-garlic paste ½ tsp.

Cooking procedure:

1. Make the dough first by combining the ingredients with enough water to form a soft dough.
2. Divide the dough into ten small balls and set aside. Then make the stuffing.
3. Now, take the dough balls one by one, flatten using a pita maker and add the stuffing in the center of the puri. Round it with your palms.

4. Prepare the instant pot and place the trivet. Arrange the balls on it and cook for 5-8 minutes until they become stiff and colored.

Easy Dal Ni Khichdi

Overall cooking time: 25 min

Serving: 4

Nutrition info: Calories: 305, Fat: 4g, Carbs: 54g, Protein: 13g.

Ingredients:

Toovar dal	1 cup
Rice	1 cup
Ghee	1 Tbsp.
Cumin seeds	½ tsp.
Cloves	2
Black pepper	5
Turmeric powder	½ tsp.
Salt to taste	

Cooking procedure:

1. First, rinse the rice and daal for 30 minutes.
2. Then, using the sauté function heat the ghee and add the cumin seeds, peppercorn, cinnamon and cloves. Sauté for 2-3 minutes.
3. Now add the rice, daal, salt, turmeric powder and 3.5 cups of water. Close the lid and manually set the time for 10 minutes.
4. Release the pressure and serve hot.

Delicious Ragi and Dates

Overall cooking time: 20 min

Serving: 1

Nutrition info: Calories: 48, Fat: 0.2g, Carbs: 10g, Protein: 2g.

Ingredients:

Whole jowar ½ Tbsp.
Whole ragi   ½ Tbsp.
Dates   2

Cooking procedure:

1. Place the whole ragi, dates, whole jowar and ½ cup of water into your instant pot. Close the lid and manually set the time for 10 minutes at high pressure.

2. Open the lid and blend until smooth.

3. Now, turn on the sauté function and cook for 2 minutes more. Stir continuously.

Masoor Dal

Overall cooking time: 20 min

Serving: 6

Nutrition info: Calories: 90, Fat: 1g, Carbs: 18g, Protein: 3g.

Ingredients:

Masoor dal	¾ cup
Oil	1 Tbsp.
Cumin seeds	1 tsp.
Asafeotida	¼ tsp.
Onion	½ cup
Garlic	½ tsp.
Ginger	½ tsp.
Chili powder	1 tsp.
Turmeric	½ tsp.
Salt and pepper to taste	

Cooking procedure:

1. Press the sauté function of your instant pot and add the olive oil. A minute later, add the onion and sauté until softened, then add the ginger, garlic, curry powder, pepper and salt. Sauté with stirring.
2. Now add the masoor dal and sauté for 2 to 3 minutes. Cover the lid and set the time for 6 minutes at high pressure.
3. When it is done, blend the dal to make it creamy using an immersion blender.

Healthy Apple and Carrot Soup with Potato

Overall cooking time: 30 min

Serving: 8-10

Nutrition info: Calories: 72, Fat: 3g, Carbs: 11g, Protein: 1g.

Ingredients:

Apple	¼ cup, chopped
Carrot	2 Tbsp. chopped
Potatoes	¼ cup, chopped
Oil	1 tsp.
Onion	1

Cooking procedure:

1. Turn on the sauté function of your instant pot. Add the oil and the onion and sauté until the onion is translucent.
2. Then add the chopped ingredients and 1 cup of water. Close the lid and set the time for 6-8 minutes at high pressure.
3. When it is done, release the pressure naturally and then blend the mixture with an immersion blender.

Dessert Recipes

Mouthwatering Rasgulla

Overall cooking time: 20 min

Serving: 16

Nutrition info: Calories: 121, Fat: 4g, Carbs: 3g, Protein: 2.7g.

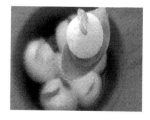

Ingredients:

Cow milk	5 cups
Lemon juice	1 lemon
Sugar	1 cup

Cooking procedure:

1. First, pour the milk into your instant pot and turn on the sauté function. When the milk is boiling add the lemon juice slowly while stirring.
2. Stir until completely curdled.
3. Take the chenna and drain the water completely. Transfer it to a muslin cloth and hang for 45 minutes for draining extra water.
4. Now add the sugar to the instant pot and pour in 4 cups of water. Heat.
5. Meanwhile, take the chenna and squeeze as much as you can and then place on a bowl to flatten. Knead the chenna 5 to 6 minutes with your palms until smooth.
6. Divide the chenna into 16 balls.
7. Then put the balls into the sugar water and close the lid. Cook for 15 minutes.
8. Remove from the heat and chill before serving.

Ginger Halwa

Overall cooking time: 20 min

Serving: 2

Nutrition info: Calories: 513, Fat: 23g,
Carbs: 24g, Protein: 8g.

Ingredients:

Grated carrot	1 ½ cups
Ghee	2 Tbsp.
Milk	5 Tbsp.
Sugar	6 Tbsp.
Grated mawa	4 Tbsp.
Cardamom	1 pinch

Cooking procedure:

1. Turn on the sauté function of your instant pot. Add the ghee and then add the carrots. Stir to mix well and sauté for 2 minutes.
2. Now add the milk, khoya and sugar. Mix well. Close the lid and manually set the time for 11 minutes at high pressure.
3. When the instant pot beeps, naturally release the pressure for 10 minutes and then do a quick release.
4. Open the lid, sprinkle the coriander powder, and mix everything evenly.
5. Serve hot.

Yogurt Custard

Overall cooking time: 35 min

Serving: 6

Nutrition info: Calories: 225, Fat: 8g, Carbs: 29g, Protein: 9g.

Ingredients:

Greek yogurt	1 cup
Condensed milk	1 cup
Fat milk	1 cup
Cardamom powder	2 Tbsp.

Cooking procedure:

1. First, take a heatproof bowl and add the all ingredients to it. Cover the bowl with foil.
2. Place the trivet in the instant pot and then pour in 1 cup of water. Place the covered bowl on the trivet. Close the lid and manually set the time for 20 minutes at high pressure.
3. When the instant pot beeps, naturally release the pressure for 10 minutes and then do a quick release.
4. Open the lid and refrigerate for chilling.

Carrot Halwa

Overall cooking time: 20 min

Serving: 6

Nutrition info: Calories: 166, Fat: 7g, Carbs: 19g, Protein: 3g.

Ingredients:

Ghee	2 Tbsp.
Raisins	2 Tbsp.
Cashews	2 Tbsp.
Carrots	2 cups
Whole milk	1 cup
Splenda	¼ cup
Cardamom	¼ tsp. (powdered)

Cooking procedure:

1. Go to the sauté function and add the ghee to it. Then add the raisins and cashews. Brown the cashews.

2. Add the other ingredients except the cardamom powder, then close the lid, and manually set the time to 11 minutes at high pressure.

3. When the instant pot beeps, naturally release the pressure for 10 minutes and then do a quick release.

4. Open the lid and sauté to thicken a little. Then add the cardamom powder and stir.

5. Eat when you want.

Kheer Rice Pudding

Overall cooking time: 35 min

Serving: 8

Nutrition info: Calories: 193, Fat: 8g, Carbs: 25g, Protein: 4g.

Ingredients:

Arborio rice	¾ cup
Evaporated milk	5 oz.
Water	10 oz.
Coconut milk	5 oz.
Splenda	6 Tbsp.
Raisins	1 handful
Cashews	1 handful
Cardamom powder	¼ tsp.
Saffron strands	1 pinch

Cooking procedure:

1. Put all the ingredients into the instant pot, close the lid, and manually set the time to 20 minutes at high pressure.

2. When the instant pot beeps, do a quick release.

3. Open the lid and mix everything.

Healthy Caramel Custard

Overall cooking time: 40 min

Serving: 6

Nutrition info: Calories: 120, Fat: 2g, Carbs: 20g, Protein: 5g.

Ingredients:

Sugar	5 Tbsp.
Water	2 Tbsp.
Eggs	3
Whole milk	2 cups
Sweetener	¼ cup
Vanilla extract	½ tsp.

Cooking procedure:

1. Take a heatproof bowl and add the sugar with 2 Tbsp. of water into it. Place the bowl over medium heat. Allow caramelizing.
2. Now take a soufflé dish and pour the caramel into it.
3. In a mixing bowl, break the eggs, and add sweetener, vanilla extract and milk. Whisk the ingredients together. Put the mixture on the caramel. Cover with foil.
4. Place the trivet into the instant pot and add 2 cups of water. Close the lid and manually set the time for 22 minutes at low pressure.
5. When the instant pot beeps, do a quick release.
6. Open the lid and refrigerate for 4 to 5 hours.

Healthy Apple Cake

Overall cooking time: 30 min

Serving: 4

Nutrition info: Calories: 160, Fat: 1g,
Carbs: 36g, Protein: 2g.

Ingredients:

Apple	2, sliced
Apple pie spice	2 Tbsp.
Muffin mix	17 oz.
Milk	½ cup
Sugar	2 Tbsp.

Cooking procedure:

1. First grease a 6-inch round pan. Then layer the apple slices along the bottom. Make sure that you are not overlapping. Sprinkle the apple pie spice over the slices.
2. Now, prepare the muffin mix and combine with milk. Pour the mix over the apple slices. Cover with foil.
3. Place the trivet and pour 2 cups of water over it. Place the foil-covered pan on the trivet. Close the lid and manually set the time for 20 minutes at high pressure.
4. When the instant pot beeps, naturally release the pressure for 10 minutes and then do a quick release.
5. You are done.

Ricotta Lemon Cheesecake

Overall cooking time: 50 min

Serving: 6

Nutrition info: Calories: 181, Fat: 16g, Carbs: 2g, Protein: 5g.

Ingredients:

Cream cheese	8 oz.
Truvia	¼ cup
Ricotta cheese	1/3 cup
Lemon zest	1 lemon
Lemon juice	1 lemon
Lemon extract	½ Tbsp.
Eggs	2

Cooking procedure:

1. In a mixing bowl add all ingredients but the eggs and mix until smooth.
2. Now break the two eggs into the bowl and then mix just to incorporate into the mixture.
3. Pour the mixture into a spring-form pan and cover with foil.
4. Now, place the trivet and pour 2 cups of water into the instant pot. Place the tin on the trivet. Close the lid and manually set the time for 30 minutes at high pressure.
5. When the instant pot beep, naturally release the pressure for 10 minutes and then do a quick release.
6. Refrigerate the cake for 5 to 6 hours.

Chocolate Cake

Overall cooking time: 40 min

Serving: 6

Nutrition info: Calories: 301, Fat: 28g, Carbs: 7g, Protein: 8g.

Ingredients:

Almond flour	1 cup
Swerve	2/3 cup
Cocoa powder	¼ cup
Walnuts	¼ cup
Baking powder	1 Tbsp.
Eggs	3
Whipping cream	1/3 cup
Coconut oil	¼ cup

Cooking procedure:

1. In a mixing bowl add all ingredients and mix until smooth.

2. Pour the mixture into a spring-form pan and cover with foil.

3. Now, place the trivet and pour 2 cups of water into the instant pot. Place the tin on the trivet. Close the lid and manually set the time for 30 minutes at high pressure.

4. When the instant pot beeps, naturally release the pressure for 20 minutes, then naturally release the pressure for 10 minutes, and then do a quick release.

Basmati Kheer

Overall cooking time: 30 min

Serving: 6

Nutrition info: Calories: 195, Fat: 11g, Carbs: 24g, Protein: 4g.

Ingredients:

Ghee	2 Tbsp.
Raisins	¼ cup
Cashews	¼ cup
Basmati rice	¼ cup
Whole milk	2 cups
Swerve	¼ cup
Water	½ cup

Cooking procedure:

1. Go to the sauté button on your instant pot. Add the oil and the cashews and raisins. Brown the cashews lightly.
2. Now add the sweetener, milk, rice and water into the instant pot and set the cooking time to 15 minutes at high pressure.
3. Release the pressure naturally. Open the lid and stir until the milk mixes well.
4. Chill overnight.

Coconut Almond Cake

Overall cooking time: 50 min

Serving: 8

Nutrition info: Calories: 236, Fat: 23g, Carbs: 5g, Protein: 5g.

Ingredients:

Dry ingredients:

Almond flour	1 cup
Coconut	½ cup
Truvia	1/3 cup
Baking powder	1 tsp.
Apple pie spice	1 tsp.

Wet ingredients:

Egg	2, whisked
Butter	¼ cup
Whipping cream	½ cup

Cooking procedure:

1. Take a large mixing bowl and mix the dry ingredients together.
2. Now, add the wet ingredients to the dry ingredients one by one and mix well.
3. Transfer the mixture to a 6-inch round cake pan and cover with aluminum foil.
4. Set the trivet into the instant pot. Pour in 2 cups of water and place the covered pan on the trivet. Close the lid and set the time for 40 minutes at high pressure.

5. After cooking, naturally release the pressure and then cool for 15 minutes. Sprinkle the coconuts, sweetener and almonds.

Breakfast Recipes

Delicious Cheese Frittata

Overall cooking time: 35 min

Serving: 4

Nutrition info: Calories: 227, Fat: 18g,

Carbs: 5g, Protein: 12g.

Ingredients:

Asparagus	½ lb.
Green onion	½ chopped
Butter	1 Tbsp.
Eggs	6
Whipping cream	¼ cup
Swiss cheese	½ cup
Salt	1 tsp.
Pepper	1 tsp.

Cooking procedure:

1. Pre-heat your oven to 350-degrees F.
2. Tenderize the asparagus with 2 Tbsp. of water in the microwave and then in a large mixing bowl, break the eggs, add the salt, milk, grated cheese and pepper.
3. Sauté the onion in the butter in the instant pot and then add the asparagus, pepper and salt. Add the eggs mixture too.
4. Now, close the lid and cook for 12 minutes at high pressure.
5. Cut the frittata into four pieces and serve.

Easy Chicken Congee

Overall cooking time: 40 min

Serving: 4

Nutrition info: Calories: 457, Fat: 22g,
Carbs: 38g, Protein: 22g.

Ingredients:

Olive oil	2 Tbsp.
Chicken thighs	1 lb.
Garlic	1 Tbsp.
Soy sauce	1 Tbsp.
Jasmine rice	1 cup
Salt	1 tsp.
Pepper	½ tsp.
Water	5 cups

Cooking procedure:

1. Simply place all the ingredients into the instant pot, then close the lid and then manually set the time to 20 minutes.

2. When the cooking is done, release the pressure, open the lid and stir to mix. Done

Healthy Broccoli, Ham and Pepper Frittata

Overall cooking time: 40 min

Serving: 4

Nutrition info: Calories: 422, Fat: 30g,

Carbs: 9g, Protein: 25g.

Ingredients:

Ham	8 oz. cubed
Sweet pepper	1 cup
Broccoli	2 cups
Egg	4
Half and half	1 cup
Cheddar cheese	1 cup
Salt	1 tsp.
Ground pepper	2 Tbsp.

Cooking procedure:

1. First grease a 6-inch pan and then place the sweet pepper in the pan and add the cubed ham. Add the frozen broccoli to cover.
2. Now, in a mixing bowl, break the eggs and add the salt, pepper and whipping cream. Whisk together, add the cheese, and stir.
3. Put this mixture into the tin too. Do not stir. Cover with foil.
4. Place the trivet, pour 2 cups of water into the instant pot and place the covered tin on the trivet. Close the lid and set the time for 20 minutes at high pressure.
5. Serve with the topping you like.

Delicious Egg Cups

Overall cooking time: 15 min
Serving: 4
Nutrition info: Calories: 115, Fat: 9g, Carbs: 2g, Protein: 9g.

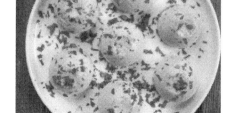

Ingredients:

Egg	4
Vegetables	1 cup, diced
Cheese	½ cup
Half & half	¼ cup
Cilantro	2 Tbsp.
Salt and pepper to taste	

Cooking procedure:

1. Take a large mixing bowl and mix all the ingredients. Pour the mixture into few ½ inch pint jars. Close the jars.

2. Place the trivet, pour 2 cups of water into the instant pot and place the covered jars on the trivet. Close the lid and set the time for 5 minutes at high pressure.

3. Open the lid and top with cilantro and sauté for 1 to 2 minutes.

Easy Cardamom Yogurt

Overall cooking time: 8 hours and 10 min

Serving: 2

Nutrition info: Calories: 386, Fat: 18g,

Carbs: 56g, Protein: 14g.

Ingredients:

Whole milk	2 cups
Whipping cream	½ cup
Splenda	5 Tbsp.
Gelatin	½ Tbsp.
Greek yogurt	3 Tbsp.
Cardamom	½ Tbsp.
Honey	1 ½ Tbsp.

Cooking procedure:

1. First, take the milk and heat it with cream for 2 minutes in your microwave. Mix the gelatin with a little warm milk and add the rest of the milk and cream.

2. Now, add the yogurt and cardamom and stir until smooth.

3. Transfer to the instant pot and close the lid. Press the Yogurt button of the instant pot and leave.

4. When done, add the honey and Splenda. Stir everything and chill for 8-10 hours.

Delicious Butter Pudding

Overall cooking time: 25 min

Serving: 4

Nutrition info: Calories: 98, Fat: 4g,

Carbs: 14g, Protein: 1.3g.

Ingredients:

French brioche bread	7 slices
Egg	2
Milk	1 cup
Brown sugar	2 Tbsp.
Vanilla	2 Tbsp.
Cinnamon	1 tsp.
Topping	as you love.

Cooking procedure:

1. First grease a 6-inch pan.
2. Now, in a mixing bowl, break the eggs and add the milk, cinnamon, brown sugar and vanilla. Whisk together and then add the bread cubes and mix.
3. Put this mixture into the tin too. Do not stir. Cover with foil.
4. Place the trivet, pour 2 cups of water into the instant pot and place the covered tin on the trivet. Close the lid and set the time for 20 minutes at high pressure.
5. Serve with a sprinkle of cinnamon and the topping you like.

Instant Pot Yogurt Whey Chapati

Overall cooking time: 52 min

Serving: 12

Nutrition info: Calories: 160, Fat: 8g,

Carbs: 5g, Protein: 12g.

Ingredients:

Flour   250gm
Yogurt whey 175ml
Olive oil   2 Tbsp.
Rolling pin   1
Pastry board 1

Cooking procedure:

1. In a large mixing bowl, mix the flour with salt. Pour in the olive oil and add whey and mix until you have a smooth and soft dough.
2. Divide the dough into 12 pieces balls and flatten each ball.
3. Place the balls into a tin and cover with foil. Place the trivet into the instant pot and pour 1 cup of water. Now place the tin on the trivet and cook for 10 minutes at high pressure.
4. Serve with other dishes.

Pongal

Overall cooking time: 20 min

Serving: 4

Nutrition info: Calories: 200, Fat: 7g,

Carbs: 22g, Protein: 4.5g.

Ingredients:

Rice	2/3 cup
Split moong	1/3 cup
Cashew nuts	20
Salt	to taste
Butter	2 Tbsp.
Hing	½ Tbsp.
Ginger	2 tsp.
Cumin seeds	1 ½ tsp.
Black pepper	2 Tbsp.
Green chili	1

Cooking procedure:

1. Turn on to sauté function and add the butter. When melted, add the Hing and ginger. Sauté for 30 seconds. Then add cumin seeds, chilies, salt and then add the moong. Sauté for 3 minutes.
2. Now add 3 cups of water and the rice. Close the lid and manually set the time for 8 minutes at high pressure.
3. When it is done, add the cashew nuts and mix.

Delicious Egg Bake

Overall cooking time: 12 min

Serving: 4

Nutrition info: Calories: 100, Fat: 0g,

Carbs: 0g, Protein: 2.7g.

Ingredients:

Egg	8
Milk	½ cup
Cheddar cheese	1 cup
Bacon	5-6 pieces, diced
Potato	2 cups, thawed
Salt	to taste

Cooking procedure:

1. Got to the sauté function and add the bacon into the instant pot. Brown for 2 minutes. Add the potatoes and cheese. Stir.
2. In a mixing bowl, whisk the eggs with salt and milk, pour into instant pot and mix well.
3. Close the lid and manually set the time for 7 minutes.
4. When you release the pressure, add salt and pepper if you want.

Delicious Giant Pancake

Overall cooking time: 8 hours and 30 min

Serving: 6

Nutrition info: Calories: 200, Fat: 5g,

Carbs: 34g, Protein: 7g.

Ingredients:

All-purpose flour	2 cups
Baking powder	2 ½ tsp.
White sugar	2 Tbsp.
Large eggs	2
Milk	1 ½ cups

Cooking procedure:

1. In a mixing bowl, combine the flour and milk. Mix until smooth.
2. In a separate mixing bowl, break the eggs and add the sugar. Whisk thoroughly and transfer it to the flour mixture. Add the baking powder and mix very well. If you do not mix thoroughly, the cake will not evenly cook and there will be some cracks.
3. Now, take a 6-inch pan and grease it with butter. Pour the mixture into it. Cover the pan completely with aluminum foil.
4. Place the trivet into the instant pot and pour in 2 cups of water. Then place the covered pan on the trivet and close the lid. Now manually set the time to 15 minutes at high pressure.
5. Allow to cook. When it is done, do a completely natural pressure release.
6. Remove the pan and transfer the pancake to a serving plate. Cut into pieces you like.

48192966R00104

Made in the USA
Middletown, DE
12 June 2019